GO FOR YOURS

GO FOR YOURS

A compilation of young, African Americans
who were brave enough to reach for the stars.

ERIKA R. MCCALL

authorHOUSE®

AuthorHouse™
1663 Liberty Drive
Bloomington, IN 47403
www.authorhouse.com
Phone: 1-800-839-8640

First published by AuthorHouse   10/11/2011

ISBN: 978-1-4670-4364-9 (sc)
ISBN: 978-1-4670-4363-2 (ebk)

Library of Congress Control Number: 2011917858

Printed in the United States of America

CONTENTS

This book is dedicated to my cousin, Ben "Tre" Gibson, whose life was taken away before he had a chance to go for his.
This one's for you!

FOREWORD

I N A recent television show, a prominent leader expressed his concern about the lack of young, African American leaders in our generation. While I agreed that you rarely see any young, African American leaders in the forefront, I couldn't help but think about the young people who are trailblazers in their communities but are rarely recognized.

A sense of disappointment came over me because too many stories are told about young blacks that consist of murder, homicide, teen pregnancy and the high HIV/AIDS rate. These negative stories have overshadowed the many accomplishments of young African American leaders of today. Leaving this current generation of African Americans to be constantly criticized. Besides having to worry about being a statistic in one of the categories mentioned above, many young people are faced with criticism from their elders in regards to the music they listen to, how they wear their clothes and the "ridiculous" jobs they seek.

These negative factors have caused many young people to turn to the media for their definition of success—causing them to get caught up in the superficial standards of what it means to be successful. As a result, they have a hard time finding their purpose and following their passion because they have a distorted vision of success. There are too many people who are not following their dreams because they feel it is impossible and have used their current circumstances as a reason to not follow their dreams. As spiritual activist Mariam Williamson politely put it:

> *"Our deepest fear is not that we are inadequate. Our deepest fear is that we are powerful beyond measure. It is our light, not our darkness, that most frightens us. We ask ourselves, who am I to be brilliant, gorgeous, talented, and fabulous? Actually, who are you not to be?*

Now, I would like to add to this quote and ask you, who are you not to be young, gifted and black? Who are you not to be as gifted and talented as Mark Zuckerberg, who co-founded Facebook, or Sean Parker who co-founded Napster? Who are you not to be young, gifted and black, when you come from a generation of people who performed the first open heart surgery (Dr. Daniel Hale Williams); led the Civil Rights Movement (Dr. Martin Luther King, Jr.); and went from working in the cotton fields to becoming a self-made business woman (Madame C.J. Walker), during a time when African Americans had fewer resources than we do now. If this is not enough to encourage you, remember you were blessed with the opportunity to see a man named Barack Hussein Obama become the first African American president; something the world thought we would never see.

My intentions are not to give you a history lesson, but to share with you some stories and examples of young and fearless African American leaders, trailblazers and entrepreneurs in this current generation. Every person mentioned, whether through a quote, example, or personal story possesses a particular attribute that led them to walking in their destiny. After you read this book, my prayer is that you are encouraged to find your purpose so you too, can walk in your destiny. *Go for Yours*!

INTRODUCTION

Go for Yours 'cause dreams come true, and this is the message we bring to you."
–Kelis, *Ghetto Children*

I F THIS is your first time reading this book, you are about to experience something so cold! You could have picked up this book for a number of reasons: you may have bought it because you heard me speak at an event, saw it on a book shelf, or you may be checking it out because you are my friend and you want to support me. Whatever made you choose to read this book, you are in for a treat.

One of my many inspirations for wanting to write a book with stories about young people who have a *Go for Yours* attitude is, Actor/Comedian Kevin Hart. I don't know Kevin personally, but I feel like I saw his career blossom right before my eyes. He has the spirit of a go-getter and exudes extreme confidence in his work. Like many stars, Kevin didn't start out in the limelight, but he seemed to be content in every stage of his life.

I had the pleasure of watching Kevin share his talent at a comedy show when he came to my alma mater, Illinois State University (ISU). When I heard he was coming to campus, I remember thinking, *he is still pursuing a career after Soul Plane?* Not because I felt he was a bad actor or that *Soul Plane* was a bad movie, but because I didn't know how I could handle the disappointment he faced during his first leading role when the movie was heavily "boot-legged"(illegally distributed and sold without permission) and was not very successful at the box office. For me, this was enough to want to pursue something else. Not for Kevin. I remember him joking about the movie during his performance.

After the comedy show, Kevin attended a party that was held for him. He was walking around, smiling and greeting everyone who came his way. He appeared to be happy and content in his current stage of life. Not knowing any better, I was thinking, *this man thinks he is doing something special.* All he did was perform in a little college comedy show and he is walking around as if he just performed in a huge show in Los Angeles. I saw Kevin a few months later in a show with comedian Rickey Smiley in another small town close to Normal and he still had the same smile on his face. Again I thought, *he thinks he is really on*! When I saw him at a bigger show in Chicago, IL, I started paying more attention to Kevin's career because I now realized that I had the wrong idea about what it meant to be successful.

I had mistaken his humility, one of the key components of **Go for Yours,** as arrogance. It dawned on me that Kevin was able to joke about something that I felt I would be embarrassed about if I encountered the same experience because he knew that failure and disappointment came with the territory of being successful. He walked around with a big smile on his face because he had a clear understanding of his purpose and was walking into it. Now I feel like Kevin understood how powerful his talent was and wasn't willing to allow anything or anyone to stop him from being less than he was destined to be.

Kevin understands what it means to **Go for Yours** and because he does, he can be found on the big screen in movies such as, *Little Fockers* or *Death at a Funeral;* or showcasing his talent on his very own television specials such as, *I'm a Grown Little Man* or *Seriously Funny* on Comedy Central. When I saw the previews for his movie *Laugh at My Pain,* I was ecstatic because it took me back to the moment at ISU when I couldn't understand why he was so happy about performing in a small college town. The title of the movie confirmed for me that the trials and tribulations he faced, shaped him into the person God meant him to be. Because of observing Kevin's road to success, I no longer have an altered view of what it means to be successful.

Go for Yours: The Definition of Success

"I want the money, money and the cars, cars and the clothes . . . I suppose, I just wanna be, I just wanna be successful."
–Drake and Trey Songz, *Successful*

S O MANY people have a strong desire to be successful but are unaware of what it really means. Some measure success by being in a position to obtain material things, others define success by how happy they are with their life. When you *Go for Yours,* you create your own definition of success. You don't allow anything or anyone define you and your desire to be successful.

So what does it mean to *Go for Yours?* Some call it grinding; others call it hustling. No matter the case, to *Go for Yours* means you don't wait for an opportunity—you create it. When you *Go for Yours* you turn your trials and tribulations into testimonies of success. People with the *Go for Yours* personality are not content with living mediocre lives. They invest in themselves and are willing to do whatever it takes to reach their goals.

This group of people more than likely birthed their ideas in a basement, garage, or their parent's house. This is because instead of working for a corporation, they want to be the corporation. They don't want to eat at the local Chinese restaurant, instead they want to travel to the Great Wall of China and eat authentic Chinese food. Most of all, they don't allow their circumstances to stop them from being the person they were created to be. In fact, they use their adverse encounters as a footstool to reach their goals.

The people I am referring to have humble spirits and come in the form of trailblazers, leaders, entrepreneurs, doctors, lawyers, athletes, and entertainers.

Now that I have given you the definition of what it means to **Go for Yours**, I want you to enjoy the stories and examples of young African Americans who were brave enough to follow their dreams and not let anything get in their way.

CHAPTER 1

THE GO FOR YOURS MYTH

"The greatness of a man is not in how much wealth he acquires, but in his integrity and his ability to affect those around him positively."
–Bob Marley

GLAMOUR does NOT equal SUCCESS

"He think he ballin cause he got a block?"
–Young Jeezy, Ballin

As previously stated, we are caught in the superficial standards of success. As a result, myths have been created about what it means to be successful. When you *Go for Yours*, don't get caught up in the hype. Success is deeper than a having a Maserati in your driveway. Besides, the people who are seen driving fancy cars and wearing nice clothes are usually the ones struggling to "keep up with the Kardashians." Also, remember success does not always mean you have a glamorous job in corporate America with your own office and administrative assistant.

President and CEO of JB Sweeping Services, Jerome Boykin, has a job that is all but glamorous, but it has brought him great success. Jerome was planning to attend graduate school at Southern University at New Orleans, when Hurricane Katrina hit. He lost all of his belongings and was left with no money.

This incident prevented him from pursuing his MBA and led him back to his parent's home and sleeping on the couch. He was also left discouraged and wondering what his next move would be.

Jerome's dad did not want him to give up and introduced him to the parking lot cleaning business. Jerome opened his mind to learn about the business and discovered it's important to keep parking lots clean because it's the first thing a customer sees when they go to the store. With the help of his dad, he invested in an industrial sweeper and started a parking lot cleaning business. Jerome landed his first contract with the local Wal-Mart in his hometown of Houma, Louisiana, and eventually landed numerous contracts with Target, Home Depot, and a host of real estate development properties.

Humbled by his success, Jerome chooses to work alongside his employees, instead of simply giving out orders. He remembers being spotted by local residents wondering why someone with so much potential was picking up trash at their local Wal-Mart. They had no idea picking up trash led him to working in a billion dollar industry, and the ability to make in one day, what some people don't make in one year. He even recalls a time when a woman outside of Wal-Mart told her children, "If you don't get a college degree, you will be outside picking up trash like him." Little did she know, he had already received a Bachelor's Degree in Business and was featured in *Black Enterprise* magazine for making $850,000 in revenues in 2008.

Jerome has developed professional relationships with his clients and prevents competition because of his quality of work and great customer service. While his intent was to just have a local business, his business has expanded to other cities within his home state, such as Baton Rouge and New Orleans.

He has also been an inspiration to others, specifically Marcus Clemmons from California, who was almost homeless after the real estate market went down. Reading about Jerome's story inspired him to contact Jerome in order to learn how to start his own parking lot cleaning business. Marcus implemented everything Jerome taught him, and as an act of "paying it forward" he opened up a homeless shelter.

Jerome may have gone to college with the vision of landing a job with a little more glamour, but his not-so glamorous job led him to achieve glamorous wealth. Don't be so quick to think wealth and success only exist in corporate America, sports, and entertainment. Open up your mind to new ideas that can provide you with the opportunity for greater wealth.

In success there are no HANDOUTS

"You better get up, get out and get something. How will you make it if you never try?"
–OutKast, *Git up, Git Out*

A MYTH WE have adopted in the African American community is the mentality of the hook-up. If you seriously want to **Go for Yours**, don't expect handouts. Work hard instead of waiting for a big time record executive to come to your town (anticipating they can get you a record deal), or trying to convince people, like Oprah, to give you money. People who wait and expect handouts will never succeed. Your blessing will not come from someone else's hard work. Every successful person worked hard for what they have, no matter where they come from, or who their family is.

Craig Wayans, Damien Dante Wayans, and Damon Wayans Jr. also referred to as the second generation Wayans, did everything but expect a handout. Coming behind family members Keenan Ivory Wayans, Damon Wayans Sr., Shawn Wayans, Marlon Wayans, and Kim Wayans, it may appear to some people that their success was handed to them. Although they reign from a family tree of comedians and actors, who have made a prominent name in the entertainment business, they had to work just as hard, if not harder, as the next person who is trying to "get on." Rather than expecting anything to be handed to them, they decided to share their talent and add to their family legacy.

Entering show business after their family couldn't have been easy. They probably had to prove to their family they were capable of maintaining their family success, and at the same time, show the world they are in the business because of their talent, and not because of their family legacy.

All three of them have worked extremely hard acting, directing and producing. Craig worked his way up from a production assistant, to writing and directing for television shows, like *The Wayans Brothers* and *My Wife and Kids*, starring Damon Wayans Sr. and Tisha Campbell. Damien went from acting in movies, like *Major Payne*, to starring in movies, such as *Malibu's Most Wanted*, starring Blair Underwood, Anthony Anderson, and Taye Diggs, and directing movies such as the Wayans family comedy *Dance Flick*. Damon Jr. has done standup comedy, had a recurring role in *My Wife and Kids*, had a leading role in the movie, *Dance Flick*, and now has a regular role on the ABC television show, *Happy Endings*. All three continue to remain humble, while consistently working toward their goals and knowing nothing needs to be handed to them.

Like Craig, Damien and Damon Jr., refuse to take the easy route by expecting hook ups and handouts. **Go for Yours** and remember nothing is owed to you. Greatness cannot be created from receiving handouts.

Hard Work does not ALWAYS result in SUCCESS

"What do you do when you've done all you can and it seems like it's never enough?"
–Donnie McClurkin, *Stand*

W E ARE often told that practice makes perfect and if we work hard, we will be successful. While this holds some truth, there will be a time when you will not reap the benefits of your hard work that you were wishing to receive. You may recall a situation, such as spending weeks completing a research paper that resulted in a low grade, putting in extra hours at work to see someone else get the promotion, or practicing a dance routine over and over again, only to be cut from the dance team. No matter how talented you are, or how hard you work, there will be people who believe your hard work is not good enough. When this happens, it doesn't mean you can't continue to *Go for Yours*.

Chicago Bears Running Back Garrett Wolfe has been playing football since he was 12, and his hard work left him with many achievements. During his final two years of his high school career at Holy Cross High School in River Grove, IL, he rushed 3,411 yards and had 56 touchdowns. He set 11 school records and earned a number of honors from Chicago media sources, like the *Chicago Tribune* and *Chicago Sun-Times.*

Garrett took his hard work to Northern Illinois University (NIU), where he became the team's starting running back during his sophomore year, and was considered one of the most productive rushers in the nation. During his 2005 season, he earned national recognition because of his performances against the Michigan Wolverines and Northwestern Wildcats.

Garrett's season was hindered because of a knee injury, and he was forced to miss three games. In spite of his injured knee, he was recognized with an All-American selection and was voted the team's most valuable player. In 2006, he accumulated 285 yards against the Ohio State Buckeyes, who was the nation's top ranked team at the time. He finished the season with an NCAA high, 1,928 rushing yards, while averaging 157 yards per game. Garrett's dedication led him to being drafted in the 2007 NFL draft's third round, with the 93rd overall selection. He became the first draft class to sign, inking a four-year deal with the Chicago Bears.

Growing up in a generation that believed that as long as you work hard, you will reap the benefits of that work, Garrett found out this is not always true. While playing professional football, Garrett learned that in the NFL, the best guys do not always get to play. If the people calling the shots deem you as incapable for fulfilling the task at hand, then you may never be given the opportunity to earn, win, or compete with the job. He has come to the realization that when it comes to professional football, your hard work does not have a direct correlation to playing time or financial opportunities, and you don't always get what you work for.

Garrett continues to work hard and is happy football gave him the opportunity to leave his neighborhood and attend college, which was something he never planned to do. He believes football gave him a platform to show the world his talents, while receiving an education and obtaining a college degree. Now, he is able to play his favorite sport for a living and earn an income that some people won't make in a lifetime. Football has opened up doors that may have been impossible to open. It has also allowed him to be in rooms with people from various walks of life and develop relationships with people he may have never met if it wasn't for football. Although Garrett realizes hard work will not always give him the results he is looking for, he puts his best effort in everything he pursues.

Overall, your hard work will lead you to great accomplishments, but there will come a time when your hard work will only take you so far. When this time arises, you must choose to be confident in your abilities and continue to **Go for Yours**.

Success can be SEEN behind the SCENES

"Solo Stars keep rocking; don't follow nobody's lead."
–Solange Knowles, *Solo Star*

GO FOR *Yours* knowing that success does not mean you will be in the forefront. One of the most important things for you to realize is that the people you see in the spotlight have people behind the scenes who contribute to their talent. These people are like the icing on the cake. Although the person in the spotlight is talented on their own, they need people to add value to what they do. The people who are behind the scenes are like the seasoning that makes something like a steak taste so good, that people keep coming back for more. They are the salt, pepper, and baked potato you need to make the steak taste even better.

Before she entered the spotlight, Solange Knowles made magic behind the scenes. Not being focused on the spotlight, she grew into her own image, not worrying about anything else—showing the world she was more than *Beyoncé Knowles' sister.*

In 2001, she broke into the music industry when she lent her voice behind the scenes as the lead singer for the animated Disney television series, *The Proud Family*, featuring Kyla Pratt. She was a featured performer on the *Austin Powers in Goldmember* soundtrack and was a back-up singer on Destiny's Child's *8 Days of Christmas* album for the song *Little Drummer Boy,* and traveled the world with Destiny's Child as a back-up dancer. Not worried about the spotlight, she was featured on Lil Romeo's song, *True Love,* and appeared in Bow Wow's music video for his song, *Puppy Love.* Solange eased into the spotlight when she debuted her album *Solo Star, which* was released in Japan before it made it to the United States.

Solange started a career in acting by starring in films, such as *Johnson Family Vacation,* starring Cedric the Entertainer, and *Bring it on: All of Nothing.* Still, she continued to make magic behind the scenes, writing and producing songs for Kelly Rowland and co-writing songs, like *Get me Bodied* and *Upgrade U,* on her sister Beyoncé's album *B'Day.* When she released her sophomore album *Sol-Angel and the Hadley St. Dreams,* it peaked at number three on the U.S. *Billboard* Top R&B/Hip Hop albums. Solange seems to realize her success is not determined by whether she is behind the scenes or in the spotlight. She helped launch Deréon, a junior apparel collection for House of Deréon, a fashion line founded by her mother and sister, and was named as an ambassador for Giorgio Armani's younger diffusion line. She promoted Baby Jamz, a hip hop-styled toy line for pre-schoolers, which was inspired by her son who enjoys hip hop music. In addition to all of her accomplishments, she has been known to rock a crowd and has been seen DJ'ing at high profile parties.

It is clear that when Solange made a career for herself, she knew success is not measured by whether or not you are in the spotlight. This allows her to remain humble when she is in the spotlight. When you watch one of your favorite movies or television shows, or hear your favorite song on the radio, remember the people who helped make it happen. Keep in mind that someone had to write, produce, direct, and create the soundtrack and design the costumes. If you think talent is only seen in the spotlight, you have the wrong idea. When you *Go for Yours,* don't get so caught up in thinking your talent has to be seen in the spotlight. Be confident your talent will take you exactly where you need to go.

You don't have to wait for Your BIG BREAK, you can CREATE IT

"Keep building up impossible hopes; impossible things are happening every day."
—Brandy, *It's Possible*

THERE IS an episode on the popular television show, *Martin,* where Martin takes his friends to Los Angeles hoping he will make his big break in the entertainment industry by being featured on the *Varnell Hill Show.* When he arrives at the studio, he is seated in the audience, and it is very obvious the host, Varnell, has no intentions of having Martin as a guest on the show. As the show comes closer to an end, Martin decides to create his own opportunity and hops on the stage while the R&B group, Jodeci, is performing. To everyone's surprise, Martin makes himself a part of the performance. This catches the attention of Varnell, who finally agrees to have him on the last two minutes of show. While this scene was intended for entertainment purposes, when you **Go for Yours,** you have to create opportunities for yourself in order to do what you are passionate about.

Internet Talk Show Host Sherhara knows what it means to create your own opportunity. Sherhara has always dreamed of a career in the spotlight and is confident she has what it takes to fulfill her dream. She was blessed with the opportunity to be in the spotlight while she was attending Indiana University. During her academic career, she developed and hosted the radio show, *Bring it On,* which is a black public affairs forum broadcast that still serves as the only radio station in Southern Indiana targeting blacks. She also hosted *Amplified*, an Indiana University student television show.

Sherhara's goal is now far beyond just wanting to be in the spotlight. She wants to ensure her passion will lead her to making a difference in people's lives. During her time at Indiana University, she headed The Black Curtain Theatre, an organization that raises awareness and appreciation of the arts, and she worked with New Being, a group that raises awareness of campus activism and social relations. She has taken her talents to the professional world and has been a spokesmodel for brands such as Cadillac, Bud Light and Extra Gum.

Upon graduation, Sherhara pursued her desire to act. She filled some roles, but after many auditions, she was often told she was good, but not what the casting directors were looking for at the time. Sherhara decided to tell herself "yes" when everyone around her was telling her "no." In 2010, she started her own Internet talk show, *The Sherhara Show,* where she features up-and-coming artists who are ready to pursue what they are passionate about. Her motto is, *You create it, and I embrace it and expose it.*

Sherhara could have continued to audition for roles with the hopes she would eventually be in the spotlight, but she decided to give herself an opportunity and fill a role she is passionate about. One of the biggest myths people believe is that they have to wait for an interview, win a competition or meet a certain person to pursue their dream. If you are passionate about doing something, create an opportunity for yourself. When you **Go for Yours** refuse to get caught up in the myths of what it means to be successful.

CHAPTER 2

GO FOR YOURS WITH A GREAT ATTITUDE AND POSITIVE SPIRIT

"The greatest discovery of all time is that a person can change his future by merely changing his attitude."
–Oprah Winfrey

EXCUSES stunt your GROWTH

"Somebody told me once that pain is a game
we all gotta play."
–Ne-yo, *I Can Do Bad*

THE ONE thing worse than having a bad attitude is being full of excuses. If you are serious about your passion and really want to **Go for Yours**, you have to throw all excuses out of the window. Not having a car, living in a bad neighborhood, or living paycheck to paycheck should not be used as an excuse to not follow your dreams. There are many people who become successful in spite of their situation. What separates them from the rest is they used their uncomfortable circumstances as an excuse *not* to fail. If you are someone who is constantly making excuses as to why you can't do something, you are preventing yourself from reaching your full potential in life.

Before he became a Grammy award-winning artist who made classic albums such as *In my Own Words* and *Year of the Gentleman, singer/songwriter* Ne-yo faced numerous obstacles that he could have used as an excuse to give up. He began his career singing in a music group called "Envy" that had a brief moment of success opening for artists like Mya and Destiny's Child. After the group was disbanded Ne-yo pursued a solo career. He worked hard creating songs and was ready for his hard work to pay off with the release of his debut album with Columbia Records. He didn't get a chance to release his first album with Columbia because he was dropped from the label.

Ne-yo continued to make music but decided to stay behind the scenes and write songs. He made his "big break" in the music industry and turned heads when he wrote the hit song *Let me Love You*, for R&B singer Mario. This song stayed on the *Billboard 100 Top Stop* for nine executive weeks. Soon after, Def Jam recordings signed him where he has released five albums, and is continuing on the road of success. Today, Ne-yo is a known as a talented artist and songwriter and was credited for the popular love ballads *Irreplaceable*, sung by Beyoncé, which stayed on the *Billboard* Charts for 10 consecutive weeks, and Rihanna's number one hit, *Take a Bow*. Apparently, Ne-yo knew his prior disappointments were not enough to stop pursuing a dream that was already rightfully his.

When you are driving on the road called success, there will always be some bumps on your journey, but don't make them be your excuse to pull over. As an alternative, put some gas in your spiritual engine, put your foot on the pedal, and *Go for Yours*. Instead of making excuses, tell yourself excuses are the tools of the incompetent, who build monuments of nothingness.

BELIEVE in YOURSELF and others will FOLLOW

"I could let these dream killers kill my self-esteem
Or use my arrogance as the steam to power my dreams"
-Kanye West, *Last Call*

ONE OF the major components in keeping a positive attitude while you *Go for Yours* is to believe in yourself. It sounds easy but this can be hard for people who grow up around negativity or are working towards a goal that seems impossible. Whatever it is you are wishing to do, have enough faith in yourself to know you are capable of achieving whatever you have set out to do. It is important for you to have faith in yourself because you will meet people who don't believe in your dream as much as you do.

In a world of entertainment filled with rejection and disappointment, Kanye Omari West was able to make himself known simply because he believed in himself. He started out as the guy to go to for fresh beats that were uniquely sampled. His vision for making beats was birthed in the city of Chicago, IL—probably in his basement. After much hard work and faith in himself, he caught the ear of many talented artists in the hip hop industry such as Jermaine Dupri, Foxy Brown, Talib Kweli, and one of his role models, Jay-Z.

Although a talented producer, Kanye had a strong desire to rap. After voicing his desire, he pursued a rapping career. Imagine how disappointed he was after being turned down by multiple record labels that had faith in him as a record producer, but not as a rapper. He was probably excited when he rapped for the first time in front of Jay-Z. Imagine his disappointment when his freestyle wasn't enough to convince Jay-Z for a record deal. Although Jay liked Kanye's freestyle and was impressed with his verse, *"Mayonnaise Colored Benz I Push Miracle Whips,"* it wasn't enough to offer him a deal with Roc-a-fella records. Being turned down by someone he admired for years was probably a hard pill to swallow and if Kanye didn't believe in his gift, he may have stopped pursuing a rapping career and kept producing music. His talent along with his positive attitude is what led him to eventually be signed with Roc-a-fella records.

His dream could have shattered when he was in a near fatal car accident that left him with his mouth wired shut but instead he recorded his first single for his debut album, *The College Dropout* with his mouth wired shut and named it, *"Through the Wire."*

Since Kanye believed in himself enough to turn triumph into a successful career, he touches the lives of many people with his lyrics by giving them something they can relate to. He has six successful albums (and counting), one with his idol, Jay-Z, 14 Grammys (and counting), and a host of American Music and Image Awards. He even started his own family and production company, G.O.O.D Music, which stands for, Getting Out Our Dreams, featuring artists like Common, John

Legend and Big Sean, which recently inked a deal with Def Jam.

Since Kanye believed in himself he has traveled the world and worked with musical icons like Michael Jackson and Elton John. Many may wonder *how can a college drop out from the south side of Chicago reach the level of success that Kanye has?*. It's because he knew the sky was the limit for him and he wasn't afraid to work towards it because he believed enough in his talent to pack his bags and move to New Jersey to pursue his dream.

Like Kanye, don't allow someone's disbelief in your dream stop you from pursuing what you believe in. ***Go for Yours*** with enough faith in yourself to keep going until you see the results you are satisfied with.

Use PASSION as your ENGINE to FOLLOW your DREAMS

"I'm going higher and higher, closer to my dreams."
–Goapele, *Closer to My Dreams*

HAVING A winning attitude, mixed with passion about your dreams, is just as important as having the skill and ability in your field of interest. Passion gives you the energy to follow your dreams, and it will make you **Go for Yours** no matter what your circumstances are. It will cause you to wake up in the middle of the night to work on a business plan, or drive miles away for an audition.

Jewelry Designer Enovia Bedford used her passion for jewelry and fashion to start her own jewelry company, Accessory Remix. At her business, she uses non-conventional items and "remixes" them into fashionable items, such as chalkboard earrings, interchangeable necklaces that become bracelets, and chain shades, which are sunglasses with a removable necklace. Enovia started out as an executive assistant in the fashion industry, scanning and sending samples to buyers. This experience made her become more passionate about using her creativity to make fashion, and she began to create pieces with discarded parts, beads and broken samples.

Enovia's passion for designing led her to the Fashion Institute of Technology, where she pursued a degree in fashion. While attending the school, she became a design assistant at a well-known fashion jewelry company. This position excited Enovia because she was on the road for moving up in an industry that she was very passionate about. Shortly after she started this job, she received news she would be transferred to the company's production department due to lack of employees. This setback was discouraging for Enovia, but she did not throw in the towel. She didn't even look for another job. Instead, she used this opportunity to learn a new side of the business, production, sales and sourcing.

All of this led to the development of Accessory Remix, where she is now selling pieces in mainstream stores. In addition to making jewelry, Enovia has remixing sessions where she takes clients' current wardrobes and shows them how to wear their clothes fresh for the upcoming season. After surviving a brain aneurysm in 2005, she decided to take her passion to another level and started to work on the development of a non-profit organization called Mini Mixes, an organization that forms a bridge for young urban girls to meet a diverse group of females that will empower them.

Enovia is so passionate about what she does that she makes the best out of every opportunity, whether good or bad. Having great passion will allow you to overcome trying times. When you face challenges, allow your passion to give you the energy to **Go for Yours.**

Do what you LOVE

"You know that feeling where everything feels right? Where you don't have to worry about tomorrow or yesterday; where you feel safe and know you're doing the best you can? There's a word for that; it's called love. L-O-V-E."
—Keke Palmer, in *Akeelah and the Bee*

DOING SOMETHING you love is more rewarding than doing something to make ends meet. When you do something you love, you have a better attitude about life in general. When you do what you love, everything else will fall into place. You may have to spend time at a job you don't like, but make sure you use it to your advantage to eventually do what you love. Until then, set some time aside to do what it is that you love to do.

Professional Football Player Randee Drew has been in love with the game of football since his dad introduced him to it at a young age. He has been playing the sport for over 15 years and hasn't stopped since. Randee's love for football grew stronger when he played for Nicolet High School in Milwaukee, Wisconsin. He spent his entire high school career on the varsity team and even filled the role as captain. Randee was an all-area player selected to play in the Wisconsin Shrine All-Star Game.

He followed his love of football to NIU where he started all four years and was one of the team captains. At NIU, Randee is considered one of the leaders in interceptions, deflections, and most games played. During his college career, he was a two-time First Team All-Conference Player and was rated the top defensive back in the conference.

Randee went on to pursue professional football and entered as a free agent in the NFL in 2004. Unfortunately, Randee was released from camp and sat out of football for the season. His love for football kept him motivated, and in 2005, he was re-signed by the San Francisco 49ers and sent to Europe to play in NFL Europe. That year, Randee broke his foot and was released again. He sat out for almost a year before he decided to play arena football in Green Bay, Wisconsin. Randee's love for football continued to grow, which led him to Canada, where he played over two years for the Montreal Alouettes, and over a year with the Edmonton Eskimos.

During his football career, Randee has torn a ligament in his finger, messed up his shoulder, broken a foot, torn his ACL, and torn his pectoral muscle. If this isn't enough, he has been cut or released a total of seven times. These setbacks did nothing but add fuel to the fire and make Randee's love for football a little deeper.

Randee's love for the game allowed him to travel around the world and encounter great experiences that he credits for building his character. He has faced times when he didn't know where his next move would be, causing him to fill roles as a teacher, football coach, and even a janitor. No matter what, he always finds his way back to his true love—football.

Try to avoid doing something just because it pays well, or you feel you need it to make ends meet. Your time is too valuable to spend it doing things you don't like to do. ***Go for Yours*** doing something that you love.

Use your imagination as a BLUEPRINT for following your DREAMS

"Sweet, sweet fantasy baby, when I close my eyes, you come and take me . . . so deep in my daydreams."
–Mariah Carey, *Fantasy*

Y OUR ATTITUDE is strongly determined by what you think, dream, and imagine. If your thoughts are crowded with negativity, you will only see negative things come to pass. There are so many people living from paycheck to paycheck because they have created an image in their mind of themselves struggling. Your imagination creates a blueprint to whatever you think. If you are brave enough to use your imagination, then **Go for Yours** with a childlike mind because children see winning results in every situation.

Young Media Mogul/Chairman of Teen Nickelodeon Nick Cannon seems to have used his imagination to create a blueprint for success. At the age of eight, he started performing with instruments his grandfather gave him. By the time he was a teenager, he landed a spot on the number one comedy club in the country, *Laugh Factory,* and a role on Nickelodeon's show *All That,* which eventually led to his own show, *The Nick Cannon Show.* He used his creativity and imagination to write for the Nickelodeon shows, *Keenan and Kel* and

My Cousin Skeeter. Nick has built a brand for himself and pursued interests, such as a music career that led to the creation of songs as fun as, *Gigalo*, featuring R. Kelly, and as serious as, *Can I Live*, a life-changing song about his mom's decision not to have an abortion when she was pregnant with him. You can see Nick's talent on the big screen in movies, such as *Drum Line, Roll Bounce*, and *Love Don't Cost a Thing*. Whether it is hosting MTV's *Wild N' Out* or *America's Got Talent*, Nick makes it happen with the spirit and imagination of a child, while not letting any obstacles get in his way.

One thing most admirable about Nick is that he uses his imagination to spread powerful messages to the youth. He portrays the message that you should embrace who you are, and he is a living witness that as long as you are comfortable with yourself, it doesn't matter what other people say about you. Nick showed the world in his freestyle mixtape, *Child of the Corn*, he doesn't care if people think he is corny; he is not ashamed of who he is. This message alone can help people overcome any self-esteem issues they may have. His heart and imagination seem to be as big as a child's, and you can find Nick supporting various causes, like the National Association of Letter Carriers' Stamp Out Hunger Food Drive, Big Brother and Big Sister's Bowl for Kids Sake and volunteering for NBA Cares.

Every day, Nick uses his imagination to create more opportunities for himself, his family, and others. He has debuted a comedy album, *Mr. Showbiz*, has a morning show on 92.3 Now FM in New York and is the manager of the up-and-coming rapper, Corey Gunz.

On a personal level, he uses his imagination to express his love for his wife, Mariah Carey, which he shared on the *Oprah Winfrey Show* telling how he proposed to her by putting a diamond ring disguised in a ring pop candy wrapper. His imagination has led to a successful marriage of four years, and counting, and beautiful twins.

Overall, Nick has been recognized for his accomplishments and was named one of the top 10 most successful young people by *People Magazine,* and he was recognized on the cover of *Black Enterprise Magazine* as one of the top 40 people under 40.

Nick started his career at a young age, and he probably didn't realize the road that was ahead of him, but it is obvious he imagined himself being great. His keen imagination took him on the road less traveled, filled with one opportunity after another.

Allow your imagination to create a detailed plan in order to achieve your goals. Take a minute, close your eyes and imagine the life you wish to have. What do you see yourself doing? What type of people will you be around? How can you get there? Once you start to imagine the things you want, you will start to see your dreams and desires come to pass.

Find HARMONY in GAINING EXPERIENCE

"You are a perfect verse over a tight beat."
–Sanaa Lathan, in *Brown Sugar*

A S VALUABLE as your talent is, your experience makes you more credible. A lot of people have an attitude that they should be paid for their talent before they have built a reputable resume. The more experience and recognition you have, the more your value goes up. Build a nice resume for yourself before you solely focus on how much you want to make or charge people for your services. *Go for Yours* realizing the value in gaining experience until you reap the monetary benefits.

When Music Producer Sam Lindley, known as "The Legendary Traxster," began producing music, he charged $25 a track. In addition to producing music, he worked at Walgreens making $400 a month. It may have made more sense for him to charge more in order to make ends meet, but he focused more on gaining experience than money, which later resulted in credibility.

Traxster started his music career rapping in various music groups and was in a group, "D 2 Tha S" (Dedicated 2 Tha Streets), which was well known in the streets of Chicago, IL. He started producing music as a necessity and used any equipment he could find to create music. Traxster innovated new ways for mixing music and recalls using a style called, "pause mixing," where he would use a two cassette tape deck as a mixer, play a song on one deck, find the part he wanted to loop, and play and pause it, while recording it on the second tape deck. Wanting to learn more about the foundation of producing music, he enrolled in college to pursue a degree in Audio Engineering. When he discovered that getting a certificate didn't guarantee a job in the field, he decided to leave school and continued to use other avenues to educate himself.

While he was still working at Walgreens, someone he produced music for introduced him to artists who were well-known on the west side of Chicago. The rap trio, *Do or Die,* became interested in his tracks, and Traxster's career took off when he produced several songs on their platinum selling album *Picture This.* He has also been recognized for introducing the Chicago artist Twista to a mainstream audience and producing multiple songs for him, including his classic song, *Adrenaline Rush.* This experience caused Traxster to be noted for making beats that complement the work of fast-paced rappers.

Traxster has built an extensive resume for himself. He co-produced Mariah Carey's song *One and Only,* that was on her hit album, *Emancipation of Mimi;* produced Ludacris' song *My Chick Bad,* that debuted at number one on the *Billboard* Charts, was certified platinum and nominated for a Grammy; and *Make a Movie,* by Twista, featuring Chris Brown that climbed the *Billboard* Charts. Traxster has made multiple platinum and gold records and has received a number of Chicago Music Awards.

He is greatly influenced by his grandfather, who passed away before Traxster was able to meet him, but left a legacy behind. He finds inspiration knowing his grandfather was a restaurant owner at a time when African Americans struggled for their rights. Traxster works hard to leave a legacy behind and shares his talent with artists and within the community. He participates in the *American Society of Composers, Authors and Publishers* (ASCAP) mentoring program and went back to his hometown to lead a song writing class at an inner-city school. Traxster believes it is important to develop your skill because talent will fail you at some point, but skill is infinite.

It is apparent Traxster knew he was "legendary," but was willing to gain experience that would allow him to reach his peak. Make sure you focus more on your gift rather than a paycheck. This doesn't mean you should allow yourself to be misused or taken advantage of, but until you build a valuable resume, focus on gaining experience. You will find that your wealth is in building relationships and gaining the exposure needed to showcase your talent.

Go for Yours with the spirit of a WINNER

"'Cause I feel like I'm running, and I'm feeling like I gotta get away . . . better know that I don't, and I won't, ever stop, 'cause you know I gotta win every day."
—Busta Rhymes, *Look at Me Now*, by Chris Brown

YOU SHOULD *Go for Yours* with the spirit and attitude of a winner. Having a winning attitude will allow you to see winning results in every situation whether good or bad. When you have a winning attitude, you are more likely to persevere in spite of the obstacles you face.

Actor Hosea Chanchez from BET's hit television show, *The Game,* is a great example of going for yours with a winning spirit. It has been stated that at the age of 20, he moved to Los Angeles, CA, to pursue his dream of becoming an actor.

In order for someone to make a move like Hosea did, they have to see winning results. Hosea may have had his doubts, and fear may have showed up a time or two, but it is obvious he was prepared to win no matter what. He took his winning spirit to California and landed roles for television shows such as *For Your Love,* starring Holly Robinson Peete. He was on two short-lived television series, *Robbery Homicide Division* and *What Should I Do,* that didn't make it past the first season, but because Hosea had a winning spirit, he did not look at these obstacles as defeat. He kept moving towards his goal and eventually landed a spot on the television series, *The Game,* as Malik El Debarge Wright, starring Actresses Wendy Raquel Robinson and Tia Mowry. *The Game* was canceled by the CW Network in 2009, but returned on the BET Network in 2011, breaking a record with 7.7 million viewers. Hosea is continuing to move up in his career with the spirit of a winner.

He is so passionate about winning that he created a non-profit foundation dedicated to the youth of America, called the Watch Me Win Movement. According to their website, www.watchmewin.org, the mission of Watch Me Win is to help aide youth in a better, more encouraged and empowered life by encouraging them to live above their circumstances. Hosea seems to believe the importance in having a winning spirit so much that he passes it on to those around him, so they can have the same spirit.

Remember a winning spirit helps you see yourself at the finish line and will get you through the difficult times you will face when you ***Go for Yours***. If needed, get rid of your fearful spirit, and replace it with the spirit of a winner and watch yourself win. Remember, true champions understand they will lose some challenges, but in the end, they will win the victory.

CHAPTER 3

GO FOR YOURS KNOWING WHO YOU ARE

"I am the American Dream. I am the epitome of what the American Dream basically said. It said, you could come from anywhere and be anything you want in this country. That's exactly what I've done."
—Whoopi Goldberg

Always "Do You"

"I make a living off of truly being myself."
—Drake, Better than Good Enough:
MTV Drake Special

You've probably heard the common phrase, "often imitated, but never duplicated." This applies to you. Part of knowing who you are is having the ability to do you. There is no one on this earth who can do you like you can. With this being said, you should never try to duplicate anyone else. When you **Go for Yours,** you will meet people who have the same interests and talents, but this does not mean you have to conform to their image. When you go against who you are, it will show.

Hip-hop artist Aubrey Graham, who the world refers to as Drake, knows what it means to "do you." Hailing from Canada and growing up in a wealthy neighborhood, he does not pretend to come from a rough upbringing to reach out to his urban audience, but he is still respected by many in the hip hop industry. Drake is able to do this because he really understands the art of "doing you." In an industry that is filled with chains, slang, and tattoos, Drake holds his own with a college boy swag, without any known tattoos, in a simple letterman's jacket, while spittin' verses he wrote on his Blackberry and using words you can actually find in the English dictionary.

People may wonder how someone like Drake can have songs with rappers who are known for rapping about drugs and living a thug life. You never hear Drake rapping about being in the hood serving dope. Instead he raps about having a "World Series Attitude," being the "go to guy for the hits right now" and telling everyone, "I'm really tryna make it more than what it is, cuz everybody dies but not everybody lives." Drake does not lie about who he is and he is respected by so many people in the hip-hop industry because he stays true to himself.

Staying true to himself allowed him to go from playing Jimmy on the Canadian teen drama, *Degrassi*, to being a well-known rapper, releasing one of the most successful mix tapes, *So Far So Gone*, which received over 2,000 downloads in the first two hours of its release. By simply doing him, Drake was signed to Lil Wayne's record label, *Young Money Entertainment*, where he debuted his highly anticipated album, *Thank me Later*, which reached number one on the *Billboard* Charts the first week of release and became platinum. He has been nominated for Grammys and has written songs for Chris Brown, Alicia Keys, and Jamie Foxx.

Doing him led him to receiving the prestigious Song Writers Hall of Fame Award, and the list goes on. Drake continues to stay true to himself, while making everything he does look cool—so cool he landed a spot on the cover of *GQ* magazine's 2010 Men of the Year issue. It is no surprise Drake makes a living by truly being himself.

When you **Go for Yours** make sure you stay true to who you are. You don't have to compromise yourself, or pretend you are someone you are not just to get what you want. Eventually, the real you will come out, so just do you.

Embrace EVERY PART of YOU

*"Listen up, I got a secret. My flaws are beautiful.
I'm way above average."*
—Raven-Symone, *Green*

WHEN YOU know who you are, it is easier to embrace every part of who you are—flaws and all. In order to *Go for Yours*, it is important that you are comfortable in the skin you are in.

The beautiful and talented actress Raven-Symone embraces who she is in every encounter. From her head down to her feet, she is not ashamed of who she is. She models extreme confidence wherever she goes and encourages others to do the same. While in the limelight at an early age, she quickly showed the world she was comfortable in her own skin when she played the innocent, but fierce Olivia on *The Cosby Show*. Raven showed us she had an attitude that could change the world, and it all started with embracing every quality she had. This role led her to receive the Young Artist Award in the category of Exceptional Performance by a Young Actress under Nine.

Raven continued to embrace herself and show more of her personality when she starred in television shows such as *Hangin' with Mr. Cooper* and *The Fresh Prince of Bel-Air*. Raven's success did not stop after she grew out of her young and innocent characters. She went on to star in various movies and television shows. You can find her in films alongside Eddie Murphy in *Dr. Doolittle* and *Dr. Doolittle 2,* and *College Roadtrip,* starring Martin Lawrence.

Raven has captured the attention of many young people and is known for her role in the Disney television show *That's So Raven.* Raven did not attempt to grow up too fast, but embraced her role on the show. She helped with its great success and led the show in becoming the highest rated and longest running series on the Disney channel. This show led to a great franchise of soundtracks, dolls, video games and DVDs.

Continuing to embrace who she is, led to another great role in the Disney channel original movies, *Cheetah Girls,* which premiered with 6.5 million viewers and sold 800,000 DVD copies, and *Cheetah Girls 2, for* which she served as an executive producer. *Cheetah Girls* created another great franchise that Raven was involved in.

Whether solo or with a group, Raven embraces who she is at every stage in her life. Throughout her entire acting career, she has also pursued a music career. At the age of eight, she debuted her album, *Here's to New Dreams,* and has released a total of five albums, including, *That's So Raven Too,* which was a soundtrack album that debuted and peaked number 44 on the *Billboard* 200.

Raven took her confidence to a new level in the movie *Good Hair,* when she shared the secret to her hair. Raven refuses to get caught up in superficial standards of beauty and models extreme confidence wherever she goes. All of this has led to her success of winning three Kids Choice Awards and Five Image Awards. In 2007, she was featured on the cover of *Ebony* magazine as the $400 million dollar woman. Raven may not have reached this level of success if she didn't embrace who she was at every step of her life.

There may be something you don't like about yourself that you can or cannot change. Whatever the case, embrace every part of you. If there is something you don't like about yourself that you are able to change, work as hard as you can to change it, but until then, EMBRACE YOU!

Know what you BRING to the TABLE

*"I hoop with the best of them, swooped up the
chest of them, dunked on a bunch, caught ally-oops
on the rest of them."*
—Fabolous, *It's in the Game*

I N ORDER to understand who you are as a person, you may need to take out the time to think about what you bring to the table. Evaluate your strengths, as well as your weaknesses, so you can show up and deliver in whatever you set your mind to do. If you don't know your assets, it will make it harder for you to **Go for Yours.**

Mic Barber knew exactly what he brought to the table when it came to being a contestant on the first season of the VH1 reality show *I Want to Work for Diddy.* Thirteen contestants were brought on the show to see who could win the competition of becoming Sean "Diddy" Combs' personal assistant. They were given various challenges, like helping Diddy sell his personal fragrance and going to London and back in one day in order to find a model. After each challenge, they faced eliminations in order to narrow down the contestant pool for Diddy's next personal assistant.

Mic was rarely up for elimination, and when he was, he used his strengths in order to capitalize on his weaknesses to allow him to continue on with the challenge of working for Diddy. Down to the last two, Diddy chose another contestant, but broke his own rule. Right before it appeared Diddy and the winner of the competition were about to fly away, leaving Mic all alone on the runway, Diddy unexpectedly selected Mic as the other winner.

Since then, Mic has continued to utilize his strengths and founded M.I.C Management Entertainment, which stands for Mastering Individual Creativity, and he manages two artists, Rich Kids and Dez'O.

Through his management company, he landed a publishing deal with Broadcast Music, Inc (BMI). Mic does a monthly A&R (Artist and Recording) showcase in New York called Mic Check Wednesdays, where he invites artists to display their talents and be recognized by A&R executives. Mic Check Wednesdays has been a success in New York, and he was recently funded for a Mic Check Wednesdays College Tour. It is clear Mic understands the importance of knowing what he brings to the table in order to get the job done. In addition to being aware of what he brings to the table, Mic strongly believes in a quote from his Uncle Leon, "If something you believe in doesn't change your life, then it's not a belief." He uses this quote as his motivation to continue on with his success.

Knowing what you bring to the table makes you feel confident in what you do. When you *Go for Yours* with confidence, you tend to hold your head up a little higher and stick your chest out a little further. Make sure you know what you bring to the table so you can embrace who you are and gain the confidence you need in order to *Go for Yours*.

CHAPTER 4

GO FOR YOURS MAKING POWER MOVES

"Nothing will work unless you do"
—Maya Angelou

Make your NEXT move your BEST move

"Make your next move your best move;
every move I make is a chess move"
—Gucci Mane, Shout Out to my Set

I F YOU are looking to succeed in your passion, you have to **Go for Yours** making moves that will make you stand out and are beneficial to your success. These moves can also be referred to as "power moves." Power moves can be putting in extra hours at work, attending a networking event, or volunteering at a local community center. Whatever the case, make sure your next move is your best move.

When it comes to the basketball court, NBA Superstar Kobe Bryant makes sure every move is his best. He made strategic moves that allowed him to go straight from high school to the professional basketball court, despite his high SAT score that showed he could have gone to college to play for Duke University, which he first intended to do. As the youngest person in the NBA at the time, Kobe made power moves that resulted in his becoming the youngest NBA starter and the youngest player to win the All-Star slam-dunk contest.

Kobe has helped the Los Angeles Lakers win five NBA championships, has played in 13 All-Star games, was the All-Star MVP four times, and is the youngest player to reach 20,000 points. He is an Olympic gold medalist known for creating shots and making moves on the court, such as the fade-away jump shot, a shot that makes it difficult for the defender to contest the shot, and the turnaround jump shot, where the player turns in the air timing the shot when the defender is not likely to jump and challenge the shot.

Kobe was recognized in *Sports Illustrated* magazine for his jab, step, and pause, a move where he jabs his non-pivot foot forward to allow the defender to relax while he pushes off of his foot to drive around his opponent and to the basket. These moves are what have led Kobe to many victories. To some it is just a game, but for Kobe, he goes to work and understands one bad move can mess up everything.

Like Kobe, *Go for Yours* making strategic moves that will get you to where you want to be. When faced with adversity, use your very own fade-away jump shot in order to make it hard for your defenders to stop you on your path. Rely on your turnaround jump shot when you are faced with a challenge that seems unbearable. If your opponents still try to prevent you from making your shot, let them relax a little, and then hit them with the jab, step, and pause, as you arrive at the basket. No matter what, continue to make power moves that will put you above the game.

Make Power Moves with the MINDSET of a CHAMPION

The Champ is here, the champ is here . . .
you can hate me I don't care.
—R. Kelly, *The Champs*

ONE OF the most valuable assets you need when you *Go for Yours* is the ability to navigate your way through trials and tribulations. The best way to do this is with a mindset of a champion. A champion is usually equipped with the right power moves that make it easier to handle any type of adversity that shows up on their doorstep. In fact, a champion welcomes the challenge because they have the ability to defeat it and are prepared for it knowing the challenge has arrived to make them stronger.

World Boxing Champion, Floyd "Money" Mayweather, Jr. has made power moves that have made him an undefeated champion. Known for knocking out his opponents, out of 41 wins, 25 were won by the way of TKO (knockout). Floyd's power move is through the popular old school technique, the shoulder roll—which is used to block, slip, and deflect his opponent's punches. When he is being cornered during a fight, Floyd simply twists his left and right foot to the rhythm of his opponent's punches.

His major power moves have led him to be a five-division world champion; winning nine world titles in five different boxing weight classes. Floyd received a Bronze Medal in the Atlanta Olympics, became a two-time winner of the International Boxing Fighter of the Year Award, also known as the Muhammad Ali Boxing Award. In 2010, *Forbes* magazine named him the second richest and most powerful athlete in the world. Whether he is defeating his opponent one jab at a time or by simply knocking them out, Floyd does not leave the boxing ring until he is undefeated. What makes him even more unique is the fact that his defensive techniques have left him with relatively few scars, which is why he was given the nickname "Pretty Boy Floyd."

If you have ever had the chance to watch a Mayweather fight, you will observe that he enjoys defeating his opponent as a smile frequently graces his face. This alone should show you that he faces each situation relaxed and ready to win. He understands that in addition to your physical abilities, defeating your opponent is all about having the right mindset.

When facing any trials and tribulations, make power moves that will leave you undefeated. Develop your own stances that will block, slip, or deflect anything that will try to prevent you from going for yours. Make jabs that will lead you towards your desired destination and don't be afraid to hit an adversity with a TKO.

SHOW people rather than TELL them

"Trash talk em, then I put em in a hefty, running down the court, I'm dunkin on em—Lisa Leslie."
—Nicki Minaj, *My Chick is Bad*, by Ludacris

WHEN YOU *Go for Yours,* allow your power moves to speak for you instead of running your mouth. There are too many people who talk about their qualities and never really show what they are capable of doing. People who are confident and serious about their talent let their actions speak for them.

WNBA Player Candace Parker seems to show people better than she can tell them. She grew up playing the sport of basketball, which is dominated by males. Instead of telling people how good she was in the sport, she showed them.

During her high school career at Naperville Central High School in Naperville, IL, Candace started in 119 out of the 121 games she played. She became the first female high school player to dunk during a sanctioned basketball game and the only player to win the *USA Today* Player of the Year Award two times.

In addition, she won the Gatorade Award for national basketball player of the year and the slam-dunk contest at the McDonald's All-American Game, where she beat top male athletes in the country, including two first round draft picks. In 2004, Candace helped the undefeated USA Junior World Championship team win a gold medal. That same year, she was invited to play in the Women's Basketball Coach Association (WBCA) High School All-American Game, a WBCA sponsored game that invites 20 of the nation's top high school female basketball players. Candace chose to show her talent, instead of talking about it, and as a result, she left her high school basketball career with a record of 2,768 points and 1,592 rebounds.

By the time she made it to the University of Tennessee, Candace didn't have to talk about her abilities because people were fully aware of who she was, and what she was capable of doing, on the basketball court. She made history again when she slam-dunked twice in one game. Candace became the Southeastern Conference (SEC) Rookie of the Year and helped her team win the SEC Tournament Championship. During the SEC Tournament Championship game, Candace was recognized for hitting the game-winning shot. She was the tournament's most valuable player and was named to the 2006 All-American Team. Candace left University of Tennessee compiling 101 wins and 10 losses.

Candace was the first pick in the 2008 WNBA Draft and was selected by the Los Angeles Sparks. In her first season, she broke the record for a rookie debut in a game, with 34 points, 12 rebounds and eight assists. She also became the second woman in history to dunk in a WNBA game and was selected to join the U.S. National Women's Basketball team in the 2008 Summer Olympics. There should be no questions about whether or not she was the MVP that year.

Like Candace, choose to show people rather than tell them. Refrain from being the type of person who always talks about what you have, what you can do, and who you know, without any concrete evidence. Don't limit your credibility by being the person who is known for being all talk, but no action.

Do what you GOTTA do to get where you WANT to be

"Happiness is hard sometimes; you gotta work for it."
—Wale, *Thug Motivation*

MAKING POWER moves can be exhausting and sometimes you may not have the energy to *Go for Yours.* There will be some things you will have to do that you may not want to do, but you must do them in order to reach your goal. Waking up before sunrise, working out every morning, studying every day for a big exam, or missing a party so you can go to work, may not be appealing, but your reward will be a lot greater than your sacrifice. These simple, yet huge factors, will take you further than you can ever imagine.

Take NBA Superstar Dwyane "D Wade" Wade, for example. It has been said he was unable to play basketball his freshman year at Marquette University due to not being in compliance with Proposition 48, which meant he did not have the GPA or SAT score he needed in high school to play ball in college. Dwyane utilized tutoring to help him improve academically because he was willing to do whatever it took to be able to play the sport he loved. The pressure of having to study and attend practice and road trips could have been enough to make him want to give up. Instead of giving up, he did what he needed to do in order to get where he wanted to be.

After Dwyane did what he needed to do, he got off of the bench and led his team in scoring, with 17.8 points per game, led the conference in steals, at 2.47 per game, and helped Marquette finish the season with a 26-7 record, which was the school's best since 1993. This was almost 10 years from the time Dwyane stepped on the court. In the 2002-2003 season, he helped his team win the first and only Conference USA championship and led them to the Final Four, which was the team's first appearance since winning the 1977 national championship. Dwyane was recognized for his performance in the 2003 NCAA tournament when he made a triple-double, with 29 points, 11 rebounds and 11 assists—making him the fourth person to make a triple-double in NCAA history.

Dwyane's exceptional college basketball career resulted in him leaving Marquette before graduation and being selected fifth in the 2003 NBA draft by Miami Heat. Since Dwyane did what he needed to do, he became the first player in NBA history to accumulate at least 2,000 points, 500 assists, 100 steals and 100 blocks in a season. He helped the Miami Heat win the NBA championship in 2006 and was named MVP that same year. Dwyane continues to be recognized for his abilities and was selected as MVP at the 2010 All-Star game.

If Dwyane did not do what he had to do, and if he chose to use his academics as an excuse to give up, we would not know him as the "D-Wade" we love to look up to. You will come across some uncomfortable situations, but you have to be willing to tough it out for the pay-off. When you give up, you are not only neglecting yourself, but you are neglecting the people who will potentially be inspired by your talent. ***Go for Yours*** with the willingness to do what you need to do in order to get where you want to be, even if it means being uncomfortable sometimes.

Step OUT of your COMFORT zone

*"Go out of your way to form friendships and
alliances with people who you wouldn't normally
encounter on your corner."*
—Kevin Liles, *The Hip Hop Generation Guide to Success*

WHEN MAKING power moves sometimes you have to step outside of your comfort zone and position yourself for opportunities that will allow you to grow and prosper. When you **Go for Yours,** you will have to go outside of your comfort zone by talking to people you may not normally talk to, going places you normally wouldn't go and doing things you normally wouldn't do.

It is obvious the beautiful and talented actress, Taraji P. Henson, was not afraid to step outside of her comfort zone in order to go for hers. It has been noted, she packed her bags and moved herself and her son from Washington, DC to Los Angeles, CA, in order to pursue her career in acting. Taraji could have chosen to stay home and be close to her family and expose her talents only in the DC area, where she was most comfortable, but she chose to step outside of her comfort zone in order to see what great opportunities were in store for her.

While she has made a name for herself in Hollywood, Taraji may still face times where she has to step out of her comfort zone in order to fulfill certain acting roles. Because she refuses to play the same role twice, she consistently steps out of her zone by starring in movies as funny as *Date Night* or as serious as *The Curious Case of Benjamin Button*, which led to an Oscar nomination. She could be singing a song with lyrics like, "It's hard out there for a pimp," for the movie, *Hustle and Flow*, or playing roles where her character wasn't the easiest to put up with, like in the movie *Not Easily Broken*, or *I Can Do Bad All by Myself*. She may have stepped out of her comfort zone for some of these roles, but you will never know because she seems to know how to make uncomfortable moments seem pleasant. Stepping out of her comfort zone allowed her to receive an Oscar nomination and multiple BET and Image Awards.

Don't be so content in your circumstances that you fail to step outside of your comfort zone in order to make power moves that lead to your reaching your greatest potential. Stepping out of your comfort zone may not seem easy at first, but be bold enough to allow yourself to experience something new.

Work CONSISTENTLY
to perfect your GIFT

"I've just been working on my game. Hopefully, you see it.
I've just been working on my shot, getting everything better
and it's coming along."
—Derrick Rose, Interview with ESPN Chicago

J UST BECAUSE you are talented doesn't mean there isn't room for improvement. There are always opportunities to take your gift and passion to a new level. When you reach your destination, don't get so comfortable you fail to continue making power moves. In reality, you should *Go for Yours* even harder because it's harder to maintain your success than work towards it.

Chicago Bulls point guard Derrick Rose is someone who consistently works on his talent, basketball. He was selected first overall by the Chicago Bulls. In his first season, he became All-Star Rookie of the year, was the first player drafted by the Bulls to score 10 points or more in his first 10 games since Michael Jordan, and was named to the NBA All-Rookie First Team. During his debut in the playoffs, he tied Kareem Abdul-Jabbar's NBA records for points scored by a rookie in a playoff debut scoring 36 points. Derrick sat out most of his second season due to injuries, but still managed to be selected to the All Star Game for the first time making eight points, four assists, and three steals. He helped his team make it to the playoffs, and in a game against the Boston Celtics, he scored 39 points.

Derrick showed basketball fans in his first two seasons that he was a talented player who possessed the ability to take his team to the playoffs. Still, he continued to work harder to perfect his skills.

It was often noted that one of his biggest flaws in basketball was the lack of a consistent jump shot. During his off seasons, Derrick continued to work on his jump shot and by his third season, he made 100 3-pointers out of 297 attempts after hitting 16 3-pointers in his first and second season. He recorded a career high against the San Antonio Spurs with 42 points, eight assists, and five rebounds. This same season he became the youngest player (age 22) in NBA history to be named the NBA Most Valuable Player. He helped his team gain over 60 wins, a first since the 1997-98 season and took his team to the NBA playoffs once again. Derrick continues to work harder as he is determined to help bring his team a championship ring.

Whatever your area of interest is, **_Go for Yours_** knowing there is always room for improvement. Continue to make power moves by thinking of innovative ways that will make your gift unique from others whom share similar interests and talents.

Go HARD, or go HOME

"People get into this lifestyle; they dream of it; they want it so bad, but when they get it, they become complacent. But, for me, it's what more can I do because it's somebody at home that wants what I got."
—Trey Songz, "My Moment" Documentary

THE ROUGH definition of insanity has been described as doing the same thing over and over again, while expecting different results. While this is true, another definition of insanity is thinking you can rest on talent alone. If you don't **Go for Yours** putting in the work necessary to nurture your talent, you may never reach the success you are hoping for. This means you have to go hard by making power moves every day until you are satisfied with your results.

Tremaine Neverson, who the world knows as Trey Songz, entered the music industry with a dollar and a dream, and he knew he "just had to make it." He did not win the Best Male R&B Artist award at the 2010 BET Awards, or go on Jay-Z's Blueprint 3 Tour by expecting to make it by talent only. Trey has gone hard since his debut album *Gotta Make it,* which sold 40,000 copies in its first week of sales and made number 20 on the *Billboard* 200. He was received well by his R&B fans, but struggled to get the attention of the mainstream community. The Recording Industry Association of America (RIAA) did not certify his debut album, but Trey continued to go harder.

By the time Trey released his sophomore album *Trey Day*, it reached number 11 on the *Billboard* 200, selling 73,000 copies during the first week, which is more than half of what he sold with his debut album. Like the first album, *Trey Day* was not certified by the RIAA. So what did Trey do? He went a little harder. Before dropping his third album, he created a buzz and released a mixtape titled, *Anticipation.* When Trey's third album *Ready* was released, it sold 131,000 copies the first week, reached number three on the *Billboard* 200, and was certified gold with the RIAA. His hard work also resulted in a Grammy nomination for best contemporary R&B album.

Trey did everything, but sit down and rest on his success; he decided to go harder and release his fourth studio album *Passion, Pain and Pleasure.* He shares on his website, www.treysongz.com, this album is more than a title for him. The passion he has for his art fuels his drive and work ethic; the pain describes the sacrifice of his personal life in order to benefit his career; and the pleasure that derives from his works and accomplishments makes everything worth it. This proves to be true, as Trey reached his highest numbers in first week sales with this album by selling 240,000 copies the first week. Trey has released numerous mixtapes in between albums, which have all contributed to his success.

If you don't believe Trey had to go hard in order to get where he is today, you may want to check him out on his *BET* 10-part documentary series, *My Moment,* which allowed his fans to see how Trey goes hard every day. Choose to go hard like Trey Songz and watch how your career will grow. When you think you have reached the peak of your success, keep making power moves and *Go for Yours* even harder. You have nowhere to move, but up.

CHAPTER 5

GO FOR YOURS BUILDING RELATIONSHIPS

"Your network determines your net-worth because your net-worth was determined by your network."
—Les Brown

It's not about WHO YOU KNOW, but WHO KNOWS YOU

"I know you from where? Elementary school?
I don't know you, man!"
—Big Punisher, *It's so hard*

T HE PRINCIPAL at your school, the vice president of the company you work for, or the pastor of your church are some examples of important people in your life you may know. While they may be someone you feel you should know, do they know you? If you were to walk up to them and say, "Hello," would they recognize your face? Would they recall your name if someone were to mention it? No matter how much talent you have, it's the people you connect with who can help you get to the next level. When you **Go for Yours**, develop relationships that allow people to know who you are and what you are capable of doing.

Siblings Brandon and Lorielle Broussard made sure people were going to know who they were when they started Barackawear, Inc. Both were working for Tyler Perry's *House of Payne* (Brandon as a screenwriter and Lorielle as a costume designer's assistant), when Brandon approached Lorielle with the idea of designing shirts in order to support Presidential Candidate Barack Obama in the 2008 election. With six hundred dollars in startup costs, Brandon and Lorielle started Barackawear, Inc. and designed *Ba-Rack the Vote* t-shirts. Their desire to increase awareness about Barack Obama made them $900,000 in revenues, allowing them to donate more than $17,000 of their proceeds to Barack Obama's election campaign.

The Broussard siblings followed the Obama campaign while selling their shirts, and even had the opportunity to meet President Barack Obama, who can probably recall seeing a *Ba-Rack the Vote* t-shirt. Their hard work and dedication allowed them to encourage young people to vote and be noticed by celebrities like Hill Harper, Will.I.Am, and a host of other well-known celebrities who publicly wore their shirts. Brandon and Lorielle made a name for themselves and were able to support a great cause. Since they have built their brand and people now know who they are, they won't have to work as hard as they did during the 2008 presidential election when they launch shirts for the 2012 presidential election. Now they are well known for what they do and have caught the eye of some investors who are interested in investing in their company.

If you haven't developed relationships with the necessary people who should know who you are, then how can they help you get to where you are trying to go? Be sure to make a name for yourself, and when you do, make sure it's in a positive way. You want the right people to know you, or know of you, and have great things to say about you.

Be BRAVE ENOUGH to go SOLO and WISE ENOUGH to know when you need a PARTNER

"I'm a movement by myself, but I'm a force when we're together."
—Ne-yo, in *You Make Me Better*, by Fabolous

O F COURSE, there is no one else who can be more motivated about your vision than you. When you **Go for Yours** a lot of your time will be spent working solo, but sometimes building relationships involves asking for assistance. You may be the driving force of your vision, but you may need help to execute your plan. There is only so much you can do by yourself, so find people you trust to assist you when needed.

When it comes to the tennis court, tennis superstars Venus and Serena Williams are brave enough to go solo, but they know when it's time for some double action. These siblings are considered two of the best tennis players who have graced the Women's Tennis Association (WTA). Venus and Serena are great when solo and even better when they are together. Both have successful careers in the WTA.

Venus is one of the most powerful baseline players, known for having one of the most powerful forehands in the WTA. She holds the record for the fastest serve struck by a woman in a main draw event and has been number one in singles three times. Venus has won 21 Grand Slam titles (seven in singles), three Olympic gold medals, and she is one of three women in an open era to have won five or more Wimbledon singles. Serena is powerful by herself, but she knows when it's time for a partner in crime, there is no one else she would call on other than her sister.

Serena is another powerful baseline player whose game is built around taking immediate control of rallies with a powerful and consistent serve. She has one of the best double-handed backhands in the WTA and can hit a winning backhand shot from any position on the court. Serena has two Olympic gold medals, 27 Grand Slam titles (13 in singles), and she has been ranked number one five times by the WTA. In addition, she is the reigning champion in singles at the Wimbledon. Like Venus, Serena knows she can do "bad" all by herself, but she knows who to call when it is time to work "some doubles."

When Venus and Serena hit the court, they are unstoppable. Together, they have won 12 Grand Slam Doubles. They are able to utilize both of their strengths in order to win. One may be stronger in one area than the other, but when they are together, you can't tell. When solo, there is no sibling rivalry because they continue to carry positive attitudes that model team spirit. They have played each other 23 times, with Venus winning 10 matches and Serena thirteen. These sisters are brave enough to go solo, but wise enough to know when it's time to work together, and together, they create the ideal team.

When you ***Go for Yours***, build relationships with people who can add to your strengths and help you move toward your vision. This also means you should share your strengths with others when they are going for their's. Whatever the situation, make sure your team is built with people who are motivated to win.

Choose your friends WISELY

"I pick my friends like I pick my fruit;
my ganny told me that when I was only a youth."
—Erykah Badu, *Apple Tree*

W HEN IT comes to building your relationships, remember to choose your friends wisely. You may have dreams that are capable of allowing you to use your talent, but surrounding yourself by the wrong people can hold you back. Hanging out with the wrong crowd and participating in activities you have no business being involved in can prevent you from reaching your greatest potential. Take time to evaluate your friendships to see if they are preventing you from following your dreams. If this is the case, try to motivate the people around you to be great, and if they aren't interested, you may have to put some distance between you and anyone hindering you from moving forward.

Dr. Rameck Hunt learned early on the importance of surrounding himself with positive people. He was born to a teenage mother and a father, who was in and out of jail, in a rough neighborhood in Orange, NJ. Both of his parents were addicted to drugs, and his grandmother raised him during most of his childhood. Rameck stayed in a lot of trouble and was what people now consider, an "at-risk" youth.

When he was 14-years old, he moved in with his uncle in a rough neighborhood in New Jersey. While attending high school, he met two friends, George Jenkins and Sampson Davis, who took a liking to him because they noticed his academic abilities. The three of them became close friends and encouraged each other to keep up with their studies. One day, Rameck was hanging out with another group of friends and was involved in beating up an older man. He woke up the next day in a juvenile detention center and vowed to never return.

That experience made Rameck realize he wanted a better life and the people he surrounded himself with could have a great effect on how his life would turn out. Rameck continued to hang out with George and Sampson, and when it was time for college, they all decided to attend Seton Hall University, a university in South Orange, NJ, that offered a program for minority students who were interested in the medical field. After Rameck received his Bachelor's of Science degree, he attended Robert Wood Johnson Medical School in Piscataway, NJ. Today, Rameck is a board certified internist at the University Medical Center at Princeton and an assistant professor at Robert Wood Johnson Medical.

He and his friends, Dr. George Jenkins and Dr. Sampson Davis, went on to write a book, *The Pact: Three Young Men Make a Promise and Fulfill a Dream.* The book is about how the three of them made a pact to find a way to attend college and go to medical school. Dr. Rameck and his friends understood the importance of surrounding themselves with people who were motivated to follow their dreams.

Go for Yours by surrounding yourself with people who look out for your best interests and appreciate who you are as a person. True friends celebrate you and motivate you to do better, instead of encouraging you to do what is not right. They can help you with situations that will change your life for better or worse, so be careful who you let get close to you. When you find friends who look out for your best interests, make sure you do the same in return.

Don't EXPECT people to always ACCEPT you for who YOU are; there may be some things you NEED to change

"You gotta be smart enough to know when to change."
—Snoop Dogg, in *I can Change*, by John Legend

IF YOU have a bad attitude, it will be hard for you to build relationships. There are some unique characteristics you have that make you the unique person you are. Then, there are also some characteristics you may need to rid yourself of if you seriously want to **Go for Yours**. Ideally, you want to be around people who accept you for the person you are, but realistically, everyone doesn't have to put up with you if you always have a negative vibe. There are too many people who walk around with a bad attitude and expect people to just "deal with it" because "it is what it is." This attitude will get you nowhere.

Model/Actress Eva Marcille was smart enough to know there were some characteristics she needed to change in order to win the Season 3 competition of *America's Next Top Model*. This top model diva went into the competition with an attitude so confident that she became offensive to others. It was clear she had the talent to win the competition, but her attitude was a turnoff to the judges and others around her.

When Supermodel and Host Tyra Banks brought this to her attention, Eva came to an understanding that although she did not come to make friends, she could still be friendly. Changing her attitude helped her win the competition, which opened doors for more opportunities. Now, she is a well-known model and actress who has graced the cover of *Essence Magazine, King Magazine* and *Brides Noir*. She is known for her role as Tyra Hamilton on the soap opera *The Young and the Restless,* and has been seen on the sitcoms *House of Payne* and *Everybody Hates Chris.* Eva's positive attitude has taken her further than a negative attitude would allow.

If there are some areas in your life where you need to change, you should do your part to make the necessary changes, instead of expecting people to accept your negative attitude, behavior, or lifestyle. Be sure to get rid of any negative qualities that are capable of bringing negativity to you, and can possibly prevent you from building great relationships.

CHAPTER 6

GO FOR YOURS READY FOR ADVERSITY

"I've missed more than 9000 shots in my career. I've lost almost 300 games. 26 times, I've been trusted to take the game winning shot and missed. I've failed over and over and over again in my life. And that is why I succeed."
—Michael Jordan

Failure is a component of SUCCESS
You can't have ONE without the OTHER

"I raise my hands, bow my head; I'm finding more and more truth in the words written in red. They tell me that there's more to life than just what I can see, oh, I believe."
—Jennifer Hudson, *Believe*

CELEBRITIES APPEAR to have it all—the money, the cars and the clothes. People watch them on television as they walk the red carpet with their expensive tuxedos and custom designed dresses, and wish they could live their lives. They have reached a point of success that allows them to walk the red carpet, go to VIP parties, and buy anything they want, but what people don't see, is the amount of failures and adversary that led to their success.

The world was able to see someone's small failure turn into a great story of success when season three contestant of *American Idol*, Jennifer Hudson, graced the stage. People fell in love with this Midwest girl hailing from the city of Chicago, IL, and immediately felt she should win. For the first half of the season, viewers saw Jennifer bless the stage when singing songs from the likes of Aretha Franklin, Whitney Houston, and Winona Judd. Jennifer faced disappointments when she had the second lowest number of votes in two of the first three shows. She was the sixth of 12 finalists to be eliminated from the show. To some, it looked like the door to Jennifer's dreams was closed. The door to winning the competition was closed, but many doors were opened.

One door closing led to Jennifer receiving a Golden Globe Award for the best performance by an actress in a supporting role in a motion Picture for her role as "Effie" in the movie *Dream Girls*. Jennifer became the first person to go from participating in a reality television series to winning an Academy Award. Another door opened when Jennifer released her debut album *Jennifer Hudson*, which won her a Grammy Award for the best R&B album and the NAACP Outstanding New Artist Award. Without failure, Jennifer may not have had the opportunity to sing *The Star Spangled Banner* at the 2008 Super Bowl, or be the first African American singer to grace the cover of *Vogue*. Jennifer lost the *American Idol* competition, but she "won" in many other ways.

She has been on tours and recently released her second studio album, *I Remember Me*, which sold 165,000 copies during its first week of release. Jennifer has also experienced many of life's ups and downs, including the unexpected loss of her loved ones. During this time, she received countless support from her family, friends, and fans, who were inspired by her faith and strength. Her strength was truly shown when she was able to continue on with her life and career and start a family with her husband and son.

You may approach a time when you feel you are close to an experience of a lifetime. If the door closes on an opportunity that seemed so promising, think about Jennifer Hudson and trust that many doors are about to open for you. *Go for Yours* by being brave enough to go through small failures in order to achieve your greatest wins.

If you CAN'T handle life's OBSTACLES, you may not be ready for your DESTINY

"They say anything is possible.
You gotta dream like you never seen obstacles."
—J.Cole, *The Autograph*

Having your computer crash after staying up all night working on a paper, losing your cell phone filled with important contacts, and working for a boss who pays you less than you work for, are examples of the small obstacles you will face when you decide to *Go for Yours*. It may seem devastating at the time, but it is through your obstacles where you build characteristics of strength, patience, and humility. Since your destiny has a purpose that is larger than life, you may approach an obstacle that will leave you wondering how something so tragic could happen to you.

U.S. Paralympic Kari Miller is a great example of someone's obstacle turning into her destiny. Kari planned on enlisting as a full time military officer, but her plans changed in the blink of an eye when she was hit by a drunk driver in a horrific car accident that resulted in the death of her friend and the loss of her legs. Before the accident, Kari was working as a production coordinator for a book and marketing publishing company, taking college courses, and serving as an army reservist. She was enjoying her position in the military because it allowed her to travel and see different parts of the world. Imagine how devastating it was when her plans changed because of one person who made a careless decision.

It would be easy for anyone to understand why Kari might want to give up on life after suffering a loss this big. She went through a period of doubt and disappointment, but she understood she still had a life to live. She also received love and support from her family, friends, and people she met through her recovery, such as her first personal assistant Toya, who tricked her into getting out of the bed for the first time after her accident.

A few years after the accident, Kari began taking classes at Parkland College in Champaign, IL, and played on the University of Illinois' wheelchair basketball team. Soon after, she was introduced to sitting volleyball, a sport she knew nothing about, but quickly gained a liking for. Kari was heavily involved in sports while growing up, but volleyball happened to be a sport she was never involved in. Kari's interest in volleyball led her to win fifth place in the Sitting Volleyball World Championship in the Netherlands, a bronze medal, two silver medals, and a gold medal for women's sitting volleyball. After transferring to the University of Central Oklahoma to pursue a degree in Biology and Veterinary Studies, she received a pair of running legs and ran her first track meet at the Endeavor Games.

Kari's personal experience taught her patience and that there is always a way to do whatever you want. Now, when she faces trying times, she remembers a Ghandi quote her first wheelchair basketball coach gave her, "Strength does not come from physical capacity; it comes from indomitable will." Kari used her obstacles as a tool to reach her destiny and continued to live her life to her fullest capacity. Her amazing story is an example that your obstacles are not a reason to give up.

If you can't handle the adverse situations that come your way, you may not be ready for your destiny. Choose to be strong enough to understand your obstacles are preparing you for your journey through life, and be ready to tackle on any adversity that comes your way. Go through life's obstacles knowing you will come out stronger and better than ever before.

In order to be MAJOR, you have to be MINOR

"Cool off, thinking we local; come on homey,
we major. We major?"
—Really Doe, in *We Major,* by Kanye West

WHEN YOU ***Go for Yours***, you must keep in mind you will have to fill minor roles and face minor setbacks that will prepare for your major role in life. In an ideal world, you would start out at the top skipping any situations of adversity and instantly become successful. Sometimes, realizing what you are capable of doing gives you the confidence to want to take on the major roles, making you think you must skip the minor roles and go straight to the top. Instead of focusing on being at the top too soon, work hard in every role you are in.

Professional Baseball Player Marcus Spencer is no stranger to filling minor roles and facing minor setbacks. His love for baseball began at the young age of five, when he had the minor role of playing t-ball. As he grew older, his love for baseball became stronger and he envisioned himself playing major league baseball one day. Marcus continued to play minor roles throughout his childhood and went on to play in college for Alabama A&M University. During his college career, Marcus faced a minor setback when he sprained his MCL, leaving him to think he would never play again. Marcus did not let this small setback discourage him; in fact, he came back that same year and played for the rest of the season. He ended his final season at Alabama A&M University with a .305 batting average and a team-best, seven home runs.

Shortly after graduation, he filled another minor role and played for a professional baseball league, the Chicago Windy City Thunderbolts. While Marcus did not want this to be his final destination in baseball, he worked hard where he was and eventually landed a seven-year contract with the Chicago White Sox. Currently, he is playing for their minor league team, the Bristol White Sox, but he continues to work hard in his minor role to prepare him for his major role. Marcus faced yet another minor setback when he broke his finger in 2010, during his first season with the White Sox. Still, he has not let this discourage him as he looks forward to upcoming seasons.

Marcus knows he is talented enough to take on the major role he is destined to be in, but he is humble enough to take on the small roles that will get him to where he desires to be. He also understands he may face more minor setbacks throughout his life and is prepared to overcome any obstacles that may come his way. While he is well on his way to living the life he dreamed of as a child, Marcus remains happy in every role and continues to enjoy his journey along the way. No matter the situation, he's going, going for his.

Go for Yours with enough humility. Take on the small roles and understand minor setbacks are merely setting you up for something major, your reward will be greater than you expected. Until then, take on the minor roles and minor setbacks with a MAJOR attitude!

Learn how to handle CRITICISM

"I see them laughin' at me, cuz my pants red, and my door won't shut, and my car's shabby."
—Bone Crusher, in *Going Thru A lot*, by T-Pain

S HARING YOUR talent can be a vulnerable feeling. In an ideal world, everyone will believe in you and your talent. This would be nice, but your gift will not cater to everyone's taste. ***Go for Yours*** with enough confidence that you will be prepared for criticism.

Singer and Songwriter T-Pain is no stranger to being criticized. He entered the music industry with a style not everyone was ready for. His choice of bright colors, mixed with crazy hats, gold chains and gold teeth to match, left room for criticism. He was highly criticized when he introduced the world to "Hard & B," a name he used for his style of songs that were recorded in auto-tone, an audio processor that corrects the pitch in vocal and instrumental performances.

His debut album *Rappa Ternt Sanga*, debuted at number 40 on the *Billboard* Charts, selling 47,000 copies in the first week. By the time he released his second album *Epiphany*, which was number one on the *Billboard* 100, T-Pain was taking over the R&B and hip hop radio stations. In 2007, his songs, *Buy You a Drank* and *Bartender*, were climbing the charts. In addition, you could hear him on tracks with popular artists, like R. Kelly, Kanye West, Chris Brown, and DJ Khalid, which resulted in him being featured on four top ten singles on the *Billboard* 100 at the same time. T-Pain's highly criticized style of music was still thriving in the music industry by the time he released his third album, *Thr33 Ringz*, which sold 160,000 copies in the first week and reached number four on the *Billboard* 200. He continued to collaborate with artists and had hit songs with Rick Ross, Ciara, and Ludacris.

T-Pain has been credited for influencing major artists to record songs in auto-tune. This use of songs was highly criticized in 2009, when rapper Jay-Z released *D.O.A (Death of Auto-Tune)*, a song that focused on the heavy use of auto-tune in songs. Despite the criticism, T-Pain still used this method to record songs and continued to make music. He was featured on the hit songs, *All I do is Win*, with DJ Khalid, and Jamie Foxx's *Blame It*, which led to a Grammy Award for Best R&B Performance by a duo or group.

In addition to music, T-Pain has entered the world of acting by having a recurring role on Fox's animated television series *The Cleveland Show*, and starring in the movie *Lottery Ticket*, starring Bow Wow and Brandon T. Jackson. T-Pain has refused to allow people's criticisms to prevent him from having a successful career and has gone on to win numerous awards, including Grammys.

Similar to T-Pain, don't allow anyone's criticism to turn into an adverse situation holding you back from achieving what you are passionate about. Learn how to handle criticism. More importantly, make sure you know the difference between negative and positive criticism. All criticism is not bad.

When you feel like you are about to SINK, choose to SWIM!

"If at first you don't succeed, dust yourself off
and try again."
—Aaliyah, *Try Again*

AFTER YOU decide to step out and ***Go for* Yours**, you will dive into an ocean filled with many opportunities. You will encounter beautiful creatures, such as fish, coral reefs, and even treasures. The same ocean full of beautiful opportunities is also filled with circumstances, like waves and wind, that result in great currents and sharks that are ready to eat you alive. When you approach an obstacle, it is up to you to decide if you will sink or swim.

It is no secret that Olympic Gold Medalist Cullen Jones chose to swim. When he was just five-years old, he almost drowned in a swimming pool. This near-death experience left Cullen with the longing to learn how to swim. At a young age, he learned that in order to overcome certain obstacles, you have to learn how to deal with them. Cullen could have chosen to stay away from the pool, but that didn't change the fact the pool would still be there, and his friends, who knew how to swim, would be having fun without him.

His decision to learn how to swim allowed him to become the first African American male swimmer to win a Gold Medal at the World University Games and the second African American in history to win an Olympic Gold Medal in swimming, period. Altogether, Cullen has collected six gold medals, one bronze medal and two silver medals in the Olympic games. In 2006, he was considered the fastest swimmer in the world. At the U.S. National Championships in Indianapolis, IN, in 2009, he set the American record in the 50 mile freestyle, with a 21.41 second completion time.

Cullen went from a little boy, who almost drowned, to an ambassador for African American swimmers determined to shatter stereotypes "one lap at a time" by spreading his message that racial and ethnic backgrounds have nothing to do with swimming abilities.

Use Cullen as an example for choosing to swim when life tosses an obstacle your way. When you dive into the ocean, make sure you swim your way through the currents, better known as disappointments, failures, and setbacks. Be prepared for the people you encounter who are like sharks awaiting you as prey. Whether you have to use a swift breaststroke or a simple doggie paddle, choose to swim your way through the beautiful ocean, which is filled with more opportunities than obstacles, one stroke at a time.

Find out who has your back when ADVERSITY comes YOUR way

"Yea, you had my back, waaaay back!"
—Kid, in *House Party*

*G*o for *Yours* surrounding yourself with authentic people you can rely on. This can be challenging because sometimes, you don't know who your friends are until you are in need of their support. It's a sad reality but the people who are always screaming, "Yea, that's my boy," or "I will ride or die for that girl," sometimes end up being the ones you don't see when problems arise in your life.

If you don't believe it, talk to Professional Football Player Michael Vick. As a star football player for the Atlanta Falcons, he was loved by many, but soon found out everyone wasn't his friend in 2007, when it was reported he was involved in an illegal dog fighting operation headquartered in his Virginia home. As soon as people found out about this incident, they forgot about all of the passes, interceptions, and touchdowns he made throughout his very successful career. He was suspended without pay, required to pay back most of his signing bonus, had his endorsements taken away, and was left with the fear he may never be able to play in the NFL again.

Michael's support and motivation to get back on track during this difficult time in his life may have come from the people who believed in him and stood by his side, despite what he did. This allowed him a spot back on the NFL roster after serving his prison time. Immediately after being released, he worked hard and was soon signed by the Philadelphia Eagles. He discovered people still cared about him after he received the Ed Block Courage Award, which is given to selected players in the NFL who are voted by their teammates for modeling inspiration, sportsmanship, and courage. After his comeback, he became the first player in NFL history to get 300 passing yards, 50 rushing yards, four passing touchdowns and two rushing touchdowns in a game. It was the love and support from family members, true friends, teammates and his fans that allowed him to get back in the game and make history.

When you face adversity it is important to surround yourself with people who genuinely care about you and will love you in spite of your faults. They will let you act a fool, tell you that you are wrong and still want to be around you. It's not too often when you find someone who knows you are liable to mess up at times and still wants to be your friend. When you meet people like this, be sure to keep them around.

CHAPTER 7

GO FOR YOURS KNOWING HOW TO HANDLE COMPETITION

"In order to succeed, your desire for success should be greater than your fear of failure."
—Bill Cosby

Use your *COMPETITION* as your *AMBITION*

"I'm not afraid of nothing, I just like the challenge."
—Lebron James, *Inside Hoops*

E VERYDAY SEEMS like a competition; we compete in sports, compete for jobs, and even for relationships. It is normal to be nervous when you are competing for something, but don't let it prevent you from following your dreams. Instead, use it as your motivation to **Go for Yours,** working diligently towards your goals.

If anyone knows the pressure of competition, it's the co-host of BET's *106 & Park*, Terrance J. When BET started their nationwide "New Faces Search" in order to find the new hosts for *106 & Park*, they received over 5,000 applications. This amount of applicants probably made some people stop in their tracks before they even started the application process. Terrance J was probably nervous when applying for the position, but he did not let competition scare him away from pursuing his dream; instead, he continued to audition. Terrance J didn't focus on the amount of people who were auditioning for the same role. He used his energy, took all of his savings, and flew to New York to audition. When he wasn't satisfied with his first audition, he rented a car and drove to Atlanta to audition again.

The competition probably became more intense for Terrance J when it was narrowed down to 10 contestants. He may have been more nervous when he found out some of the contestants had experience in commercials and professional radio. While he may have been nervous, apparently he knew his experience was just as valuable as the people he was competing against. Terrance J, a graduate from North Carolina A&T, who once was the president of the Student Government Association, a DJ for the campus radio station and had pledged Omega Psi Phi Fraternity, Inc., knew he had something to offer the show.

When Terrance J won the role of a *106 & Park* co-host, along with Rocsi Diaz, they were compared to the previous *106 & Park* pairs, Free and AJ, and Big Tigger and Jalissa. Instead of viewing this as more competition, Terrance J and Rocsi used their beautiful personalities to gain love from their fans. Today, *106 & Park* has been on the air for over 10 years, and Terrance J has contributed much to their success.

He continues to be humble in his role and takes every opportunity to use his popularity for great causes. He was chosen by McDonalds to be the ambassador of their African American Future Achievers Scholarship Program, where he travels to 10 schools in the New York tri-state area. He has co-hosted the *106 & Park* weekend countdown and has appeared on MTV Video Music Awards in Japan. Not being afraid of competition allowed him to pursue an acting career, and Terrance J can be spotted in the movie *Stomp the Yard 2*, and the BET television show *The Game.*

When you **Go for Yours** in a particular area of your choice, expect to have a little competition. If someone else gets whatever it is you were competing for, congratulate them and be thankful you were qualified enough to be considered in the running. Also, remember there is enough success to go around for everyone, and you will end up where you are supposed to be.

STAY in YOUR lane

"Bouncing on the highway, switching four lanes, screamin'
through the sunroof, 'money ain't a thang.'"
—Jay-Z, *Can't Knock the Hustle*

*G*o *for Yours* by staying in your lane and not putting too much focus on your competition. When you focus too hard on what's going on with the next person, you make your endeavors seem less valuable. You can also be thrown off track from what you are pursuing. Spend time focusing on you and what you are accomplishing. It's okay to observe people and learn how they strategize in order to make themselves successful, but you should never put too much focus on them.

Nobody knows how to stay in their lane better than Rapper/Mogul Shawn "Jay-Z" Carter. He entered the music industry in his own lane when he decided to create an independent record label with Damon Dash and Kareem Biggs after he couldn't get a record deal from any major record labels.

Under this label, he debuted his classic album *Reasonable Doubt,* which is considered one of the "500 greatest albums of all time" by *Rolling Stone magazine.* Not stealing anyone's style of rapping, he created his own way of rapping and doesn't mind rapping either fast or slow. Since his debut, he has sold over 450 million records, including hit albums *Hard Knock Life*, *Blue Print*, *The Black Album* and *American Gangster*, and is the recipient of 13 Grammy Awards, and counting. Jay-Z is one of the most dissed hip hop artists, but has stayed in his lane and has not entertained every artist who attempted to beef with him because he knows they aren't worth his time or money.

In addition to his music career, Jay-Z is a successful businessman who brings buzz to every company he puts his hands on. He seems to have a vision and a plan that he sticks with, and does not let anyone get in the way of what he is doing. Most importantly, Jay-Z doesn't worry about what anyone else is doing. Because he is able to mind his *own* business, he continues to build opportunities for himself that have created *more* business.

In addition to being a co-founder of Roc-a-fella Records, he is the co-founder of the urban clothing line, Rocawear, that makes $7 million dollars in annual sales. In 2007, he sold the rights for $204 million, but still retains his stake in the company and oversees the product development. He is the co-brand director for Budweiser Select, and he collaborates on marketing programs and creative advertising development.

Jay-Z is also a co-owner of the popular sports bar 40/40, which has been located in New York, Atlantic City, and Las Vegas, and he is one of the co-owners of the NBA basketball team, the New Jersey Nets.

He was the CEO of Def Jam Recordings until he became the head of Roc Nation, an entertainment company and music label, which includes artist, songwriter, producer and entertainment management.

Roc Nation is known for emerging artists J. Cole, Jay Electronica and Willow Smith. Most recently, he published *Decoded,* a memoir described as an intimate, first-person portrait of the life and art of Jay-Z, organized around a decoding of his most famous and provocative lyrics. All of this led to Jay-Z being considered as one of the 100 most influential people in the world by *Time magazine.*

If Jay-Z spent more time wondering what other people were doing with their careers, he may only be known today as being just another great hip hop artist, instead of the rapper who went from the Marcy Projects in Brooklyn, NY to one of the most successful hip hop artists and business moguls ever born, with a net worth of $450 million.

When it comes to your own success, be like Jay-Z and stay in your own lane and mind your own business. Like "Jiggaman" said in his song, *Heart of the City (Ain't No Love),* "What you eat, don't make me s#@!." So why worry about what other people are doing?

Your ONLY COMPETITION should be YOURSELF

"You act like I just got up in it, been the number one diva in the game for a minute."
—Beyoncé, Diva

I N THE end, the only competition you should have is yourself. There is nothing wrong with a little competition that will motivate you to be the best you can be, but that should not be your primary focus. Instead of competing with others around you, try to compete with who you were the day before. The more you focus on competing with whatever others are doing, the more you lose sight of what you are doing.

When it comes to competition, it does not exist for the R&B Diva Beyoncé Knowles. She started her solo career performing as if there was no competition, and eventually became her only competition. You may be wondering how Beyoncé can have no competition. Think about it, when she releases a new album, do you compare her to other singers, or the previous albums she released?

Her sophomore album *B'day* was not compared to other artists who released their albums that year, but it was compared to her debut album *Dangerously in Love*, which awarded her five Grammys. Along with *B'Day*, she gave her fans *The Beyoncé Experience Live*, which showed her performance during her worldwide tour in Los Angeles. Continuing to compete with herself, *Beyoncé* gained the same amount of Grammys for her album *I am . . . Sasha Fierce,* as she did for her debut album.

As a solo artist, she has brought home 13 Grammys; she was the first female artist to be awarded the International Artist Award at the American Music Awards; and was listed as the most successful artist of the 2000's decade by *Billboard. Beyoncé is one of the best-selling music artists of all time and has sold over 75 million records. An article in The Washington Post stated she soars above her imitators. This is an example of having no competition. The closest person to competing with Beyoncé is Sasha Fierce, her on-stage alter ego. Beyoncé created this alter ego that is strong and fierce while on stage, which is why she has been credited for her extraordinary performances.*

Beyoncé has taken her talent to the movie screen, as she was featured in movies like *Austin Powers, Cadillac Records,* and *Dream Girls,* where she was nominated for two Golden Globes. This is why there is no competition for *Beyoncé.* If she focused only on outshining other artists around her, she may not have reached the level of success she is at today.

Instead of trying to compete with everyone else, ***Go for Yours*** striving to be better than you were the day before. Don't focus on outshining others, focus on being the best you, and eventually, you will be your only competition.

CHAPTER 8

GO FOR YOURS WHEN FACING DIFFICULT PEOPLE

"Throughout life people will make you mad, disrespect you and treat you bad. Let God deal with the things they do, cause hate in your heart will consume you too."
—Will Smith

Be willing to APPROACH confrontation

"I'm leaving the swine, verbal vegetarian; squashed beef with Ice Cube; came in this rap life nude; now I'm fully clothed with flows."
—Common, *Hungry*

WHEN YOU *Go for Yours*, you will approach situations and people you may not necessarily agree with. No matter how much positive energy you put out, there will be someone who will try to make it difficult for you to move ahead. When this happens, be open to confront the issue instead of letting it linger. Confronting people about a situation can be discomforting, and sometimes, fearful. Although it may not be one of your favorite things to do, make sure you approach situations before they get out of hand. Tell the person what you are mad about, and don't take the weak route some people take when they air their grievances by updating their Twitter and Facebook statuses, only hoping people indirectly get the message. This is a bad idea! There are more ideal ways to confront situations without welcoming the possible drama that can come along with it.

When Emcee/Rapper Common released his classic joint, *I Used to Love H.E.R*, a song that talks about the changes in hip hop between the late 1980's and early

1990's, it resulted in a small beef with the Westside Connection. Common's efforts to raise consciousness caused the Westside Connection to release a song called *Slaughter House,* that mentioned Common's name. Common, in return, made a song called, *The B**** in Yoo.* Before it became too much, Minister Lewis Farrakhan, the highly regarded leader of the Nation of Islam, stepped in to help them "squash" their beef. When Common released his classic song, his intentions were probably far from wanting to start a battle. Since he didn't mean any harm, Common could have refused to sit down and diffuse the situation. However, if he wasn't willing to address this confrontation, it may have escalated to a more unnecessary and nastier battle.

Since this confrontation, Common has gone on to become a successful Grammy Award winning artist known for making classic albums such as, *One Day it Will All Make Sense, Electric Circus, Like Water for Chocolate, Be, Finding Forever* and *Universal Mind Control.* He is known for his positive lyrics and for bringing positive energy to every show. Common holds his "side card" as an actor and can be seen in movies among actors such as, Denzel Washington, Queen Latifah, and Morgan Freeman. His positive vibe makes it easy for him to be well-respected in the movie and hip hop industry. The small dispute he had with the Westside Connection did not prevent him from having a lasting career in entertainment.

More recently, Common approached a small confrontation when he was asked to perform at the White House's music series, "Evening of Poetry." Conservatives were against him performing at the White House, claiming his lyrics promoted cop killing and violence towards the former president, George Bush. Common responded to this controversy in a positive way and went as far as writing a comment on his Facebook page that described his love and support for police officers and troops. Common clearly understands the importance of approaching confrontation in order to continue moving forward.

Sometimes you will have to approach confrontation so you can move on to bigger and better things. Small disagreements, like the one Common experienced, will give you "common sense" to handle the larger disputes you will approach during your road to success. If you avoid confrontation, it eventually builds up, and you may end up taking it out on the wrong person, or exploding when you finally release it to the person you have the problem with. When you come across confrontation, approach the issue before it gets out of hand so you can continue to **Go for Yours.**

Keep NEGATIVE people at a DISTANCE

"I gotta question, why they hatin on me? I ain't did nothing to 'em, but count this money and put my team on; now my whole click stunning."
—Soulja Boy, *Turn My Swag On*

T HE BEST way to handle difficult people is to keep them at a distance. *Go for Yours* surrounding yourself with positive people who celebrate you and appreciate you for the person you are. Keep people out of your circle that can potentially block you from the adventure of obtaining what you desire.

DeAndre Cortez Way encountered a variety of negative people when he introduced the world to Soulja Boy, also referred to as "Soulja Boy Tell Em." Although there were millions of fans around the world cranking that Soulja Boy, there was a large amount of people who criticized him for killing hip-hop and making ring-tone music with no message. Soulja Boy refused to allow negative comments prevent him from making party-themed music that makes people want to get up, dance, and have fun. He also didn't allow the harsh comments made about his music prevent him from being the trailblazer he set out to be.

If people spent less time hating on Soulja Boy, they would have found that he is a young, smart entrepreneur who, before the age of 21, self-published his first single "Crank that Soulja Boy," and promoted the song by using innovative marketing tools such as YouTube and MySpace. He used these tools to create a following and self-publish his own music. Independently, Soulja Boy released his own album, *Unsigned and Still Major: The Album Before Da Album* along with a low budget video that showed the world how to do his dance. *Crank That* topped the *Billboard* Charts as well as the Ringmasters Charts, ranking in ringtone sales. His song was a great success and he received a Grammy Nomination for Best Rap Song at the 50th Grammy Awards.

This still wasn't enough to convince some people who still referred to Soulja Boy as a one-hit wonder. Soulja Boy kept all negative people at a distance and showed the world his "*Pretty Boy Swag*" and continued to have everyone's "*Speakers Going Hammer.*" In 2010, Soulja Boy made the *Forbes* magazine Hip-Hop Cash Kings List, reporting to have made $7 Million in 2009. All of which would have been impossible if he had focused on negative energy.

When you cross paths with negative people, remember to keep them at bay. Leave the haters, nay sayers, and dream killers out of your reach and continue to ***Go for Yours***.

Rise ABOVE hurtful WORDS

"I am so comfortable in the skin I'm in; I'm secure about who I am, so you go ahead and talk all you wanna. I built up a shell and it's hard as armor."
—Kandi, *Fly Above*

T HE POPULAR phrase we learned as a child, "sticks and stones may break my bones, but words will never hurt me," is far from the truth. Words have the power to make or break you as a person. Unfortunately, everyone has experienced being ridiculed by someone at least once in their lifetime by someone who lacked confidence in themselves, and in return, tried to make someone else feel bad. Don't allow people's hurtful words to prevent you from seeing how valuable you are.

If anyone knows about being ridiculed, it's the former supermodel and dynamic entrepreneur, Kimora Lee Simmons. At the age of 10, she stood at 5'10"—surpassing the height of her fellow peers. Her growth spurt led her to being bullied and teased. In order to boost Kimora's confidence, her mother enrolled her in modeling classes at the age of 11. She was soon discovered at a model search in Kansas City, MO, and was sent to Paris to model. At the age of 13, Kimora received a modeling contract with Chanel. She became a sensation in the modeling industry and modeled in fashion shows, such as Karl Lagerfeld's Haute Couture show, as a child bride and graced the covers of many magazines.

Eventually, Kimora took her talent to the fashion industry, and alongside Russell Simmons, she created the clothing line, Baby Phat. As creative director and president of the clothing line, Baby Phat went from baby t-shirts to a line of urban women's clothing. In 2004, Kimora and Russell Simmons sold the apparel and licensing for $140 million and started to expand the line by developing the Simmons Jewelry Company and the "Diamond Diva" line. That same year, they created a line of women's fragrances under the Kimora Lee Simmons brand. In 2005, the Simmons Jewelry Company and Sanrio launched a licensing partnership called the "Kimora Lee Simmons for Hello Kitty."

Through modeling and fashion, Kimora has discovered more talents and taken them to the television and movie screen. She appeared in the movies *The Big Tease, Beauty Shop,* and *Waist Deep.* She earned a Tony Award for working as executive producer of the series, *Russell Simmons Presents: Def Poetry Jam,* and has been a judge for model and fashion-based television shows, such as *American's Next Top Model* and MTV's *Fashionably Loud.*

In addition, she has her own show, *Kimora: Life in the Fab Lane,* a reality show on the television network E!. The show takes a look into the life of Kimora. She even published the book *"Fabulosity: What it is and how to get it."* It is obvious Kimora did not allow hurtful words from her childhood to prevent her from following her dreams into adulthood. Now, she is able to approach every encounter with the same confidence she spreads to others, specifically her children Ming, Aoki, and Kenzo.

You can't control what people say about you, but you can control how you react to negative and hurtful words. Keep in mind that people say and do hurtful things because they aren't happy with themselves. Also, make sure you aren't the person saying negative and hurtful words to, and about, other people. ***Go for Yours*** remembering words have the power to uplift someone, or bring them down.

Let your HATERS be your MOTIVATORS

*Banks told me go 'head and switch the style up; if they hate
then let them hate; just let the money pile up.*
—50 Cent, *In da Club*

*G*o *for Yours* allowing your haters to be your
motivators. Most people hate on others in order
to make themselves look and feel better. What they
don't know is, when they hate on someone else, they are
subconsciously giving that person praise. Your haters
can ultimately help lead you to your success. Your haters
may think they are setting you up for destruction but
they are really pushing you towards your success. This
is why it is important for you to know how to handle
them.

Nobody knows about haters more than Curtis "50
Cent" / "Fifty" Jackson. It is obvious he had plenty of
haters because before he decided to leave the drug game
and pursue rap, he was shot at and struck nine times.
Known for having a number of feuds with well-known
rappers, he uses these feuds to make major moves in
the rap game. Fifty has used his haters as his motivation
to create unduplicated success. His debut album, *Get
Rich or Die Tryin',* hit number one on the *U.S. Billboard
100* and sold 872,000 copies the first week, eventually
selling six million copies.

When his sophomore album *The Massacre,* was released, he sold 1.4 million copies in the first week; it was certified platinum five times, and he received a Grammy nomination for the best rap album. Fifty was ranked by *Billboard* magazine as the sixth best and most successful "Hot 100 Artist" of the 2000-2009 decade, as well as the number one rap artist during this decade. He continues with his successful music career and has worked on a number of projects that allowed him to "let the money pile up."

He expanded his career and hit the big screen starring in films like his semi-biography, *Get Rich or Die Tryin',* and *Home of the Brave,* alongside actor Samuel L. Jackson. From G-Unit Clothing to doing voiceovers, when it comes to making money, Fifty does not let haters get in the way. He was a representative for Vitamin Water and worked with Glacéau, the company that created Vitamin Water, to develop a new drink called Formula 50. He has a stake in the company, and when Coca-Cola purchased Glacéau for $4.1 billion dollars, *Forbes Magazine* estimated Fifty earned $100 million dollars from this deal after taxes. Fifty couldn't make these kinds of moves if he was worrying about haters.

The best thing you can do to your haters is ignore them. If they are not worth your time or attention, don't even bother to entertain them. Instead of wasting time worrying about your haters, let them motivate you to work harder. Continue to be kind to them, and in the end, those enemies will become your footstool.

While on the subject of haters, **don't let your BIGGEST HATER be YOURSELF.** Sometimes people spend so much time focusing on their imaginary haters that they ignore the biggest hater of all: THEM. You may be wondering, how can I hate on myself? This can be done in many ways: focusing too much on others, not believing in yourself, or bringing too much negative attention, is how. For example, when you hear someone giving a shout-out to their haters, do you ever wonder whom they are referring to? In reality, they are bringing negative attention to themselves. Anything you do that can bring negative energy your way is an example of hating on yourself. Don't let that be you.

SOMETIMES you WILL be MISUNDERSTOOD

"Misunderstood ain't gotta be explained."
—Lil Wayne, *Don't Get it Misunderstood*

H AVE YOU ever found yourself in a situation where your intentions were good, but your actions were not perceived well? Your intent to get your point across can sometimes result in people getting offended or upset. When you go against the "norm," be prepared for controversy and criticism. As long as your actions don't result in anyone's life being in jeopardy, **Go for Yours**, and stand for what you believe in.

American Cartoonist Aaron McGruder, of the controversial animated series *The Boondocks*, is no stranger to facing difficult people. *The Boondocks* started out as a comic strip at Aaron's alma mater, University of Maryland, and soon turned into a popular comic strip featured in over 250 publications. The comic strip has been briefly pulled from various newspapers because of its satire and was highly criticized after the September 11, 2001, attacks when one of the main characters, Huey, called a government tip line to report Ronald Reagan for funding terrorism.

Now, it is a popular television show on the *Cartoon Network's* adult-oriented cable television network, *Adult Swim,* starring actors John Witherspoon and Regina King, and has still been misunderstood in many ways. The show is about two young boys, Huey, who is strongly influenced by social justice leaders, and Riley, who is influenced by African American contemporary pop culture. Huey and Riley move from Chicago to the suburbs (The Boondocks) with their granddad. *The Boondocks* is filled with controversial characters like Uncle Ruckus, a self-hating black man and has raised concern from prominent figures regarding episodes such as *The Hunger Strike*, where Huey refuses to eat until the television network *BET* is off the air and *Return of King*, where Dr. Martin Luther King, Jr. awakens from a coma and is so upset he calls black people "trifling, shiftless and good for nothing."

Aaron has been criticized for his use of the "N" word, and he does not have the best reputation with some television networks and political figures. *The Boondocks* was named one of the top ten controversial cartoons of all time by *Time Magazine*. Although misunderstood, he continues to highlight certain situations happening in the African American community by adding comic relief mixed with the reality of what is going on in our generation. Many people have misinterpreted Aaron's intentions, but he does not allow it to get in the way of speaking his mind and getting his message out. Currently, *The Boondocks* has completed three successful seasons, and Aaron has not let the fact that people don't always agree with him stop his success.

At the end of the day, how ever good your intentions are, there will be a time when you are criticized or ridiculed. When this happens, continue to remain positive and continue to **Go for Yours**, even if it means being misunderstood.

CHAPTER 9

GO FOR YOURS AND
PAY IT FORWARD

"If you learn late, you pass it on to people so they can learn early."
—Russell Simmons

Think about what you can GIVE, instead of what you can GET

"Givin' back to the children of tomorrow
for good karma today."
—Ludacris, *War with God*

N O MATTER how much money you make, or how successful you become, true happiness comes from the gift of giving. Whether it is in the form of food, clothing, time, or money, being able to give to others is a true blessing. With this in mind, you should *Go for Yours* thinking about what you can give, instead of what you can get. It's easy to think about how much money your gift or talent can bring, but when you enter a situation thinking about what you will receive, you are blocking the true blessing that comes from giving. If you focus more on giving than receiving, you will plant a seed for greater rewards to come.

One person who seems to truly understand the gift of giving is Rapper/Actor Chris "Ludacris" Bridges. He entered his career with the spirit of giving when he interned at Hot 107.9 FM in Atlanta, GA. If you are familiar with internships then you know interns usually work for free or for a small stipend. He gave his time, and in return, he eventually held down the number one spot on evening radio and received an opportunity to share his talent of rapping on promotions for the radio station. Ludacris planted a seed that led him to signing with Def Jam Recordings and becoming well known in the music industry, releasing popular albums such as *Back for the First Time, Word of Mouf* and *The Red Light District.* At the time, Ludacris may not have realized volunteering his time could lead to three Grammy Awards, nine BET Awards, three MTV Video Music Awards, and an American Music Award. If he focused on getting paid immediately for his talent, he may not have had the successful rap career that led to him acting and starring in movies like *Hustle & Flow, 2 Fast 2 Furious,* and the groundbreaking movie, *Crash.*

On another level, Ludacris used his celebrity status to create the Ludacris Foundation. According to the foundation's website, www.theludacrisfoundation.org, "the Ludacris Foundation strives to inspire youth through education and memorable experiences to live their dreams by uplifting families, communities and fostering economic development." Their three areas of focus are Leadership and Education; where children are challenged to map out their goals, Living Healthy Lifestyles; which encourages them to focus on living a healthy life and Ludacares; where Ludacris sponsors a toy, food and clothing drive and back to school program. In addition, the foundation has two campaigns, the Runaway Love Campaign, a campaign that increases national awareness about the issues of runaways, and a HIV/AIDS awareness campaign. The Ludacris Foundation has been recognized for its efforts and received a Community Service Award from the city of Atlanta and the Spirit of Youth Award from the National Runaway Switchboard.

Ludacris appears to be the gift that keeps on giving. He hosts a weekend called Luda Day Weekend, which is filled with fun and amazing parties featuring celebrity guests. Although this weekend is meant for fun, he does not forget to give. During a Luda Day Weekend in 2009, he and the Ludacris Foundation partnered with Nissan South to give away 20 used vehicles to support people in need. That same year, heavy rain led to a widespread flood across the state of Georgia, causing $250 million in damage. Ludacris and his friend, the Atlanta native rapper, T.I., joined together and raised over $100,000 to help Atlanta flood survivors. Ludacris understands the gift in giving, and he receives so much in return.

Like Ludacris, don't get so caught up in thinking about what your success can bring you, that you don't think about how it benefits others. You can't be blessed if you aren't a blessing to others.

It's not ALWAYS about YOU

"I betcha think this song is about you"
—Janet Jackson, *Son of a Gun*

T HERE ARE certain things in your life that you will naturally desire. People are often taught if they have faith, they will get the desires of their heart. While this is true, it is necessary for you to understand that what you desire, is not always about you.

President/CEO of Preppy Gyrl & Company LaToya Ausley always had a love for lip gloss. Her love for lip gloss grew because of the fact she had to wear a uniform at the private school she attended. Her uniform made it hard for LaToya to express herself, so she used hair and lip gloss to make her personality stand out. When LaToya's favorite lip gloss discontinued, she had a hard time finding another one that suited her. She thought it would be nice if she could create her own lip gloss, but because of lack of funds, she pushed the idea to the side. A few years later, her husband, Donell, encouraged her to give the idea of creating lip gloss more thought.

LaToya researched what products go together and decided to purchase some products. After playing around, she started making and wearing her very own custom-made lip gloss. LaToya wanted to make lip gloss just for her to wear, but her friends became interested in the product. She would invite them over for Sunday dinner, and they would tell her what kind of lip gloss they wanted her to make.

LaToya's friends were approached by inquiring women who wanted to know where they purchased their lip gloss. Her friends referred them to LaToya, and she began to get phone calls from women interested in buying her product. At this point, she hadn't thought about going into business because it was just something she liked to do. The growing interest in her product forced her to come up with prices for her lip gloss. The word quickly spread, and LaToya began to do parties for women, allowing her to make them custom-made lip gloss. The parties were a success, and LaToya started booking parties on a regular basis.

The overwhelming response caused LaToya to teach some of her friends how to make the lip gloss. When parties weren't enough to satisfy her customers, she opened a lip gloss boutique in Chicago, IL, and named it Preppy Gyrl and Company because of her love for academia. LaToya's interest in lip gloss turned into a boutique where women could not only receive custom-made lip gloss, but excellent service. She sought to create an atmosphere that was inviting, where people left feeling rejuvenated from their experience. On the day of the grand opening, LaToya expected just her family and friends to show up. To her surprise, there was a line of people wrapped around the corner waiting to get lip gloss from her new boutique. They waited hours for lip gloss, and she stayed open two hours later than expected. By then, it was no secret that Preppy Gyrl & Company had a purpose of its own.

LaToya's love for lip gloss turned into her purpose. She is able to use her desire to help woman embrace who they are by letting them know they are beautiful and unique. At Preppy Gyrl & Company, LaToya treats her customers more like personal clients, and she mixes the textures and flavors of their choice in order to give them a personalized lip gloss that is fitting to their personality. The boutique has expanded, and now Preppy Gyrl has a clothing line, in addition to lip gloss. LaToya used her Catholic girl fashion background to create oxfords, polo's, and tote bags. LaToya's success proved her passion for lip gloss wasn't just about her.

Like LaToya, you have certain desires that will allow you to pay it forward by sharing your talent with the world. Remember, there is purpose in the things you desire. If you don't believe it, think about some of the things you once desired that never came to pass. You may no longer desire it because there was no purpose behind it. *Go for Yours* thinking about what it is you desire and how it can be a benefit to others.

Encourage others to be GREAT

*"Five in the air for the teachers not scared to tell
those kids livin in the ghetto that the people holdin
back that the world is theirs."*
—Lupe Fiasco, *The Show Goes On*

ONE OF the most rewarding experiences you will get while paying it forward is through mentorship. The thought of being able to help change someone's life in a powerful way is a feeling that cannot be explained. Once you have reached your goals, be sure to serve as a mentor to someone who looks up to you and may want to follow a similar path.

Joshua Mercer, founder of Swish Dreams, a sports and education foundation, is great at encouraging others to be great. This Howard University graduate was led to volunteer with local youth when he learned about Chicago's Englewood communities' lack of financial education, high rates of illiteracy, and high violence rates. Eventually, he founded Swish Dreams, where he mentors kids by using their love for sports to allow them to achieve success in other areas, such as math, science and life skills. Through Swish Dreams, Josh has served over 250 students and has developed relationships with many prominent organizations.

As a teacher in Chicago, IL, he has contributed to the growth and development of many students he mentors. Joshua led students to a first place finish in the city of Chicago's Youth Business Plan Competition, The Chicagoland Entrepreneurial Centers Future Founders Business Plan Competition and the Chicago Urban League's Investor Entrepreneur program competition. Although his intention is not to be recognized, he was named one of the top 40 game changers under the age of 40 by the Urban Business Roundtable in Chicago, and he has been featured on *WGN News* for his efforts to be an encouragement to others.

Like Joshua, ***Go for Yours*** encouraging others to be as great as they can be. Speak words of encouragement to people you encounter in your daily life, especially those who look up to you. A kind gesture or word of encouragement can go a long way. Spend time mentoring someone and share with them what you did to become successful so they can be encouraged to be just as successful as you are, if not more.

ASSIST and SUPPORT people on their WAY to VICTORY

"Win or lose . . . We gonna walk out of this stadium tonight with our heads held high."
—Denzel Washington, in *Remember the Titans*

AS STATED before, when you **Go for Yours**, you should mentor to others around you. There are many ways you can mentor someone. For some people, you may serve as a mentor only in the time of need, and for others, you may have to mentor to someone on a regular basis. Mentorship is very powerful when someone is pursuing a goal. If you are blessed with the chance to mentor someone while they are following their dream, provide them with assistance, if needed, and support them in any way possible.

Collegiate Football Coach Rod West seems to have a passion for assisting people on their way to victory. He uses his love for football to coach and mentor young men. Rod's first mentor was his father, who he recalls making him watch Sports Center instead of cartoons during his childhood. This experience resulted in the love for football and playing the sport for 15 years. Rod served as a mentor to his peers when he held the position as the captain of his football team at Selma High School in Selma, AL. He went on to play for Alabama State

University, where he is credited for his 89 tackles and three interceptions during his collegiate football career. Rod left Alabama State, graduating cum laude, with a degree in English and a minor in Political Science.

He was accepted into law school, but his love for football gave him the desire to coach. Instead of pursuing a law degree, Rod moved to Kentucky to coach for Kentucky Christian University. During his time in Kentucky, he served on the defensive coaching staff and finished second in the nation for fewest passing yards per game. This experience led Rod to Delta State University in Cleveland, MS, where he was on the staff that advanced on the Division II National Championship Game. At 24, Rod is the youngest coach for Texas A&M Commerce and is responsible for the defensive backs.

Rod understands the influence a coach can have on their players and feels his coaches did a great job in recognizing each player was different. He can recall a particular coach having a great impact on him because he constantly critiqued and challenged him. Rod understands every player wouldn't have responded to this method of coaching the same way he did, which is why he uses different coaching techniques with each player. He enjoys mentoring his athletes and talking to them about their aspirations, as well as any personal issues they may have. Rod understands the pressure his players are under, and from his own experience, he knows how it feels to be a young athlete away from home for the first time. One of the most important lessons he teaches them is to forget about yesterday, don't think about tomorrow and just focus on today.

There are so many people who have potential and don't know it because they didn't have someone who believed in them when they shared their dreams. Like Rod, your mentorship may be just what a person needs in order to reach their goal. Whether it is through mentorship, or sharing your talent so that others feel good about themselves, make sure you ***Go for Yours*** understanding the importance of paying it forward.

CHAPTER 10

GO FOR YOURS
MOVING FORWARD

"You cannot change the past but your future is spotless."
—Rev Run

A painful PAST does not prevent a POWERFUL FUTURE

"Let's stop looking at how bad things are and focus on how well they may go."
—Malik Yusef, *Promised Land*, featuring Adam Levine and Kanye West

S OMETIMES YOUR past makes it hard for you to move forward and encounter new and rewarding experiences. You can't control who your parents are and how they chose to raise you. You also have no control over some of the things that happened to you during your childhood. Unfortunately, some people have experienced a childhood filled with physical and mental abuse, rape, molestation, and many other disappointments. Situations like this can make people feel like their future is not so bright. If this relates to you, keep in mind, no matter how rough your upbringing was, you can still **Go for Yours** and fulfill your purpose.

Grammy Award Winning Spoken Word Artist Malik Yusef did not let his painful childhood prevent him from living a fulfilling life as an adult. While most children grew up with mothers who nurtured them and told them they could be anything they wanted to be, Malik's mother replaced hugs and kisses with punches that eventually resulted in a broken nose and many bruises. Instead of encouraging her son, she told him he wouldn't amount to anything in life. Growing up in an abusive home was more than enough for a child to handle, but he was also diagnosed with the learning disability dyslexia, that can hinder a person's ability to read, write, spell, and sometimes, speak. Malik did not receive the love he needed from his mother, but found love on the streets when he joined a Chicago gang. He experienced many situations that could have resulted in him being dead or in prison, but there was a purpose in his life that was beyond his control.

Eventually, Malik developed a love for poetry and received recognition when he helped Actor Larenz Tate in his role in the movie *Love Jones*, when he played the poet, Darius Lovehall. This opened up more doors for Malik to explore his talent. He was seen on Russell Simmon's HBO show, *Def Poetry Jam*, performing his notable piece, *I Spit*. Malik collaborated on a script for *Hollywood Jerome*, a short film adaptation of one of his poems that consists of the tale of a 14-year old Chicago Southside gang member who idolizes classic Hollywood gangsters caught in a police standoff.

Malik's talent has expanded to the musical scene. He has released two albums and has collaborated with other artists, such as Raheem Devaughn, Common, John Legend, and Kanye West, who has made Malik a part of the G.O.O.D Music Family. He received Grammy awards for his work with Kanye West and John Legend and has received the Chicago Music Award for Best Poet from 2002 to 2008. Malik is a noted poet, artist, writer, and musician who has taken his talent across the world, and he did not allow his painful past to prevent him from his successful future.

If a situation from your past is hindering you from moving on to your successful future, take the steps necessary to heal your wounds. Utilize resources, such as counseling and spirituality, to help you with the healing process and don't dwell on the past.

Remind yourself that your past is not your fault, and no matter how bad you were treated in your past, you survived it and were placed on this earth to fulfill a purpose. Once you are healed, help others who are in similar situations. Don't be ashamed of a past you had no control over. Also keep in mind, you are at a greater advantage because your past experiences made you strong enough to face the negativity and disappointment that come with following your dream.

Don't let your MISTAKES
hold you HOSTAGE

"In order to survive, you gotta learn to live
with regrets."
—Jay-Z, *Regrets*

D WELLING ON your past mistakes can make it hard for you to embrace new opportunities. There will be times in your life when you wish you hadn't made a certain decision, or when you said something you can't take back. The hardest part of making a decision you wish you hadn't made is living with it. Instead of focusing on your mistake, use it to your advantage to do better. Do not allow your past mistakes to prevent you from seeing what is in store for you in the future.

HIV/AIDS Activist David D. Robertson was devastated when his doctor told him he was living with HIV. This diagnosis changed David's life, and he eventually lost his job, his nice apartment, and probably some of his "friends". A situation like this is enough to make you want to give up, but instead of wallowing in regret, David found purpose in his mistakes. It was through this experience where he learned he is a gifted and talented speaker, and now he is able to enlighten people, specifically the youth, about the pandemic of HIV/AIDS by telling his story.

David refused to let his mistakes hold him hostage. He continued on with his life by pursuing a bachelor's degree in Sociology and Communications and working as a featured blogger for *Poz.com*, an online magazine that focuses on health, life, and HIV. He was featured on MTV's *Staying Alive,* started a campaign called The Face of H.O.P.E (Helping Other People Evolve) and released his documentary entitled, *H.I.V.* (*Helping Innocent Vessels).* David continues to spread the message about HIV/AIDS and has stated he strongly believes his purpose is to talk to as many people as he can about the disease because if he doesn't, "their blood will be on his hands." In other words, he feels if he doesn't share his story when he has the opportunity, he will feel responsible for the lives of people he had a chance to talk to before they contracted HIV/AIDS. David realizes the decisions he made in the past don't have to prevent him from living a healthy and happy life now.

Keep in mind, you can't change the mistakes you've made, but you can learn from them in order to become a better person. If you can accept the things you can't change, you will realize your purpose is often revealed through your mistakes. **Go for Yours** without letting your past mistakes hold you hostage.

Paint a beautiful PICTURE
of your SUCCESS

"Painting pictures with my mind,
making memories using my eyes."
—Adele, *Painting Pictures*

H AVING A clear vision of your goals can help you move forward and walk into your destiny. Sometimes your vision gets blurry because of your circumstances or people around you who don't believe in your dream. If you want to prevent yourself from allowing anything to distort your vision, use your imagination to paint a beautiful picture of success. Sometimes it is hard to move forward because your vision has been distorted. Going for yours involves having a vision. Your vision will give you the energy you need to follow your dreams and help you get through the times when you want to give up. Paint the picture you want to see and don't let anyone distort your vision.

It took a lot of experiences before the emerging artist, Dana Todd-Pope, decided to paint the picture of what she wanted to be in life and accept her calling as an artist. Since pre-school, she knew she was talented. At the age of three, she recalls her teacher asking the class to draw a self-portrait. While her classmates drew stick figures of themselves, Dana drew a very detailed self-portrait. Her teacher was so impressed she shared the portrait with Dana's classmates and teachers in the school. After many compliments, she realized drawing was something she was good at, and she developed a desire to become an artist.

Dana's passion for art grew but her picture became faded when her grade school teacher told her art was a hobby, and not a career. She internalized those words well into her adult life and became fearful of pursuing art as a full-time career. While Dana was attending the University of Illinois, pursuing an engineering degree, she bought a paint kit with her book voucher money and decided she wanted to learn how to paint. Her very first painting was a portrait of her best friend, which she gave to her as a birthday gift. Dana continued to paint from time to time, but she always remembered her teacher's comments.

Dana left college and moved to New York to pursue a modeling career. When modeling jobs weren't coming fast enough, she would sit in her Brooklyn, NY, apartment and paint. One of her friends saw her paintings and told her she should sell them. Dana hadn't given selling her paintings much thought, but she took them to Prospect Park in Brooklyn and laid them out in the grass. People in the park who were interested in buying her paintings approached her, but she was still fearful about becoming an artist and decided not to sell them. However, the fact that people liked her paintings helped build her confidence.

When Dana was ready to sell her paintings, she sold her first two to her good friend, Singer and Songwriter Anthony Hamilton, whose career was just beginning to take off. Dana's pictures were later featured in

Anthony's music video, *Charlene*. At this point, Dana was confident in her talent, but continued to pursue her modeling career. She found an agent and moved to Los Angeles, CA, to model and attend fashion school. Dana's modeling career began to take off when she did a photoshoot for the talented photographer, David LaChapelle. Her career continued to grow, and she did photoshoots with high profile celebrities, like the singer Kelly Clarkson. Although her career was flourishing, Dana and her fiancé moved back to Chicago, IL, when she found out she was pregnant with her daughter. This resulted in her putting her modeling career on hold and trying to figure out her next move.

When she moved back home, Dana would wake up in the middle of the night thinking about selling her paintings. She joined a seven-week entrepreneurship program at her church, called "A.R.I.S.E" (To Actively Raise and Inspire Individuals to Build Businesses with Excellence), that awards the top 10 participants seed money for their business. Dana did not win an award, but it gave her the confidence to go out and sell her paintings.

Dana got over her fear of rejection when a lady from her church asked her about her paintings. She explained she was still scared to put herself out there. The lady responded, "You will not live a defeated lie." These words gave her the confidence she needed to take her paintings to the popular Chicago art gallery, Gallery Guichard, to see if they would be interested in displaying her paintings. When she walked in, Dana approached the owners, Mr. & Mrs. Guichard, and one of their business partners. After showing her paintings,

Mr. & Mrs. Guichard were so amazed that they took two paintings and gave her a contract that day.

A month later, Dana's paintings were displayed in the New York National Black Fine Arts Show. She sold one painting, and the other was selected for Macy's special show in their Herald Square store. It took years for Dana to accept her calling and realize it was okay to go down the path of art. Today, her art has been sold around the country. She has shared her art in many forms and is in the process of publishing a children's financial literacy book she has written and illustrated. Dana has decided to paint her own picture for her life and fully accepts her calling as an artist.

When it comes to painting your personal life picture, be creative as possible. Add as many colors and hues as you want. If you are not talented enough to paint your picture, create a vision board. When someone tries to discourage you along the way, remember the picture you painted and continue to ***Go for Yours***.

Don't GIVE UP on your Dreams

"If you look in the sky, and you don't see your dream . . .
man, don't get defeated, cause,
and trust me you can build it."
—Pharrell Williams, in *Lavish*, by Twista

T OO MANY people refrain from following their dreams because they don't believe their dreams can come true, making it hard for them to experience something great. The harsh realities of life can make dreams seem so far away and difficult to move toward. This causes people to continue to dream without working toward their goals.

Chicago Fashion Mogul Lavelle "V-Dot" Skyes, co-owner of Succezz, a gym shoe and clothing boutique located in Chicago, never gave up on his dream of becoming "succezzful." He was born in the Robert Taylor homes on the south side of Chicago, in an era when the "dope boys" were hot, and young black men went from playing football to killing each other. Growing up, Lavelle always had a love for fashion and sneakers, and he remembers receiving Nike catalogs in the mail. Lavelle approached many situations that could have prevented him from believing it was possible for his dreams to come true. In high school, his best friend was killed in the hallway while at school, and another friend went to prison for committing murder. In order to escape, he moved to the north side of Chicago to live with his aunt.

Lavelle dropped out of high school and began to sell drugs. While living with his aunt, he was in a car accident that had the potential to leave him paralyzed, but instead, he was in a body cast for eight months. He ended up moving back to the Southside and got his first job at a popular sports apparel store where he frequently shopped.

He decided to get his General Education Degree (GED) and attend Southern Illinois University (SIU). While attending school at SIU, Lavelle received news from home that one of his close cousins was shot in the head. He came home for the funeral and never went back to SIU.

When he returned back to Chicago, Lavelle asked for his last job back, and seven years later, he was running the sports apparel store. By then, Lavelle made a nice living for himself, but he had a larger vision of partnership. Wanting to take his career to another level, Lavelle asked if he could receive partnership in the store. Instead of receiving partnership, his pay was cut, and he was asked to change the way he dressed. He was used to wearing stylish attire that would attract customers to the clothes in the store. Lavelle complied with the changes, but made a decision to quit after a sale went wrong, and the controversial money was to come out of his paycheck. That day, Lavelle decided to follow his dream of owning his own store, and he quit that same day.

Lavelle didn't have any knowledge about starting a business, so he went to the library and taught himself how to write a business plan. He opened his first store, Self-Conscious, and soon after, a second store, Encore, which was ironically, the old sports apparel store where he previously worked, but was now going out of business. Lavelle sold both stores before he opened up Succezz, with NBA Basketball Player Bobby Simmons. They came up with the name, "Succezz," because of their desire to be successful. They added the z's on the end because they felt obtaining success sometimes means a lack of sleep. Lavelle's fashion sense and Bobby's NBA career make their store stand out from others.

In addition to fulfilling his dreams, Lavelle wants to help people reach their dreams, and he believes he has the ability to pick winners out of a crowd. He wants to help enhance people's talent, open multiple stores and pursue a career in music. Lavelle is a motivational speaker and has spoken at various universities in Chicago. He strongly believes life is what you make it, and you shouldn't let anyone stop you from what you want to do; you are the only one who holds yourself back.

Similar to Lavelle, never give up on your dream. When you find yourself wanting to give up, close your eyes and envision yourself being exactly where you want to be. Then, open your eyes and **Go for Yours** until your dream becomes a reality.

Continue the LEGACY

"They say hip hop was gone, then everybody mourned; imma pick it up where they left off and respawn."
—Diggy Simmons, *Shook One*

A NOTHER FORM of moving forward is by continuing the legacy that was handed to you. This generation has been handed a torch from our elders, with a great responsibility to make the best out of the opportunities they fought for African Americans to have. *Go for Yours* by being part of a legacy that will have a positive impact on generations to come.

Vanessa, Angela, Jojo, and Diggy Simmons, who are the offspring of the infamous hip hop legend, Joseph "Rev Run" Simmons, from the rap group Run DMC, chose to continue their family legacy. They decided to add to the legacy of their father and uncle Russell Simmons by following their passion and purpose that would keep the Simmons' family legacy alive. Together, sisters Vanessa and Angela launched Pastry Footwear, which has evolved from fashion sneakers to apparel and accessories.

Individually, Vanessa has started a career in acting and modeling. She appeared on the soap opera, *Guiding Light,* and in independent films, *Speed Dating, Boogie Town,* and *Dysfunctional Friends.* Angela worked as the executive director for *Word Up! magazine,* and teamed up with the magazine to start *Angela's Rundown,* a mini magazine featured in *Word Up!* Jo Jo has pursued a music career with his music group Team Black Out, and Diggy has also pursued a career in music, and his career took off when he released a YouTube video rapping over the Nas song, *Made You Look,* which received over two million views. This led to his being signed with Atlantic Records and releasing his mixtape, *Airborne.* He performed at the 2011 BET Awards, where he was nominated for the Young Stars Award and participated in the Closer to My Dreams Tour. These siblings have added to their family legacy and have served as an example for the next generation, specifically their younger siblings, Russell and Miley. ***Go for Yours*** moving forward in the name of your ancestors, elders, and family members who have paved the way for you to obtain what is already rightfully yours.

CHAPTER 11

GO FOR YOURS WITH SWAG

"I'm extremely ambitious. I don't know why people are afraid to say that. I won't sell my soul to the devil, but I do want success and I don't think that's bad."
—Jada Pinkett Smith

CONFIDENCE is the key to "SWAG"

"Heartthrob neva, black and ugly as eva; howeva, I stay
Coogie down to the socks."
—Notorious B.I.G., *One More Chance*

T HE WORD "swagger" has been around for years; this generation has taken the word and given it a little flavor as we now refer to it as "swag." So what does it mean to have swag? According to Jay-Z, he "invented swag, poppin' bottles puttin' supermodels in a cab." This verse alone should tell you that swag is all about how confident you are with yourself. Swag comes within; you cannot buy it off the shelf or obtain it by having materialistic things. In order to **Go for Yours,** you must be confident in who you are as a person. This does not mean you have to be arrogant or cocky, but you should not allow other people's views of you determine how you feel about yourself. You should be so content with who you are, that it doesn't matter if someone thinks you are ugly or cute, dumb or smart.

One thing most admirable about the late rapper, Notorious B.I.G is he was confident in who he was. He was said to have stood at 6'3", weighing as much as 300 to 380 pounds. You probably could have called him any name in the book, but he wouldn't have cared because he had so much confidence in himself. In fact, he released his demo tape under the name Biggie Smalls, which was a reference to his childhood nickname. His confidence even rubbed off on others when he had men of all ages and sizes singing, "I love it when you call me Big Poppa." Biggie loved who he was, and that made others love him.

Biggie did not let the opinions of others stop him from following his dream of rapping. He made it clear that people used to doubt him when he wrote his song, *Juicy*, regarded as one of the greatest rap songs of all times. In this song, he approaches the people who doubted him when he says, "Considered a fool, 'cuz I dropped out of high school." He did not allow other people's opinions of him stop him from making classic albums like *Ready to Die*, which his fans still listen to and which was certified platinum four times. His confidence also led him to receive *Billboard* Music Awards for Best Rap Artist of the Year and Rap Artist of the Year for his song, *One More Chance*. Up until his death, Biggie didn't let anyone stop him from being who he was, and because of that, he is considered one of the greatest rappers of all time.

Confidence attracts people. No one wants to be around someone who always doubts themself and what they can do. If you focus too much on your flaws, you may be discouraged to fulfill your dreams. At the end of the day, it doesn't matter what other people think; they don't have to walk in your shoes and they definitely aren't paying your bills. Don't allow other people's opinions of you affect your self-esteem. Instead of spending time trying to please others and make them like you, spend time appreciating you.

STREET SMARTS and EDUCATION go HAND in HAND

"I'm opposite of moderate, immaculately polished with a
spirit of a hustler, and a swagger of a college kid."
—TI, *Live Your Life*

A s STATED before, swag comes from within.
One of the major components of maintaining
your swag is through your intellect. There is nothing
like being able to entice someone with a captivating
conversation or educating people about something you
are knowledgeable about.

This is why street smarts and education go hand in
hand. There are some things in life that you can only
learn through experience, and for others, you will learn
through education. People who have street smarts are
aware of what is going on around them and can benefit
from their knowledge. When they mix their street
smarts with education, they are able to effectively back
up what they know. Street smarts can only take you so
far, and vice versa. You may be thinking, there are a lot
of millionaires who made it without an education. It is
true there are many successful people without formal
education, but if you do your research, you will learn
they are educated in the area they are successful in.

Rapper David Banner is a great example of someone who has street smarts, as well as an education. When he was young, David educated himself by learning how to play instruments like the keyboard and second hand drum. His street sense led him to a part time job at a local grocery store that assisted him in funding his interest in music, where he created his own music and put it on a CD to sell. David pursued his bachelor's degree in Business at Southern University in Baton Rouge, LA, where he served as the president of the Student Government Association. During his collegiate career, David formed a rap duo called Crooked Lettas and they debuted their album, *Grey Skies*. This album did not get David his big break in the music industry, but it gave him the experience he needed to continue his pursuit in the music industry.

David's music career took off while he was working on his master's degree in Business at the University of Maryland. At that time, he was using his street smarts to perform in clubs, when an executive from Universal Records noticed him. David probably used the experience he obtained while pursuing his business degree when he was offered a five-album contract and released his first album *Mississippi: The Album,* which included his hit single *Like a Pimp,* that reached number 15 on the Hot R&B/hip hop chart. David continued to release albums and make hit songs like *Get Like Me,* featuring Chris Brown and Yung Joc, and *Shawty Say,* featuring Lil Wayne, which reached number two on the rap chart.

David created the theme song for the game Saints Row, an action adventure video game that can be played on Xbox. He was credited for writing, producing, and arranging a song for the Gatorade television commercial *Gatorade has Evolved*. He has branched into acting and was seen in the movies *This Christmas* and *Stomp the Yard 2*. When it comes to David Banner, his street smarts and education seem to go hand in hand.

When you **Go for Yours**, make sure you are well educated in your area of interest. Use your street smarts to make moves where your education can't take you. There are some things in life you can only obtain or understand by having book sense, but for everything else, you better hope you have some common sense. Or, why not have both?

Use YOUR RESOURCES

"It is not good to have zeal without knowledge, nor to be hasty and miss the way."
—Proverbs 19:2

S OMEONE WHO goes for theirs with swag knows how to navigate from exactly where they are. Meaning, they don't allow issues such as lack of funding to affect them. Instead, they think of creative ways to use the resources available to them in order to get where they want to be. Keep in mind that there are various resources around you that can help you *Go for Yours.* Resources go beyond money, you can find them at school, work, the library, at the local community center and through people.

Author/Motivational Speaker Ephren Taylor brought a new definition to swag when he creatively utilized some of the resources around him. Coming from a small town of Carlisle, Mississippi with very few resources available to the community, Ephren still managed to find a way to identify resources that made him a millionaire by the age of 16. He may not have realized it at the time, but he started his career at the age of 12 at the library where he learned computer programming. He used his newfound knowledge to create a 3D video game that he sold to his friends for 10 dollars a copy.

During his adolescent years, when most kids still don't know what they want to be when they grow up, Ephren created a Windows notepad replacement program and developed software for a top worldwide nutritional supplement company.

At 17, he created a job search site for teenagers and college students called, GoFerretGo.com, which was ranked four out of 100 top companies run by teens, and is valued at over $3.4 million. By the time he was 23, Ephren was the CEO of City Capital Corporation, making him the youngest African American in history to be hired at a publicly traded company. At City Capital Corporation, Ephren was in charge of $150 million in assets.

Ephren's great accomplishments have led him to be invited as a guest expert on local and national television shows. He appeared weekly on FOX news, and he has been featured on ABC's *20/20* and *The Montel Williams Show,* and radio shows, like the *Doug Banks' Morning Show*. He also hosts his own radio show that airs on the XM Satellite Radio Station, Family Talk 170XM called, *The Soul of Success*. Ephren has served as a panelist for the Wall Street Economic Summit and the Congressional Black Caucus. He launched a 15-city "Urban Wealth Tour" that promotes economic empowerment, affordable housing, and entrepreneurship in urban communities. The purpose of this tour is to bring private investors, educators, non-profit organizations, religious institutes and government forces together to create a positive change in urban communities.

He serves as a resource through his books and is the author of the best-selling book *Creating Success from the Inside Out,* where he teaches what it takes to succeed in life by following your own path and refusing to be defeated. He also wrote the book entitled *Elite Entrepreneur,* in which he shares how to master the seven phases of growth to take your business from pennies to billions. He has earned the Kansas Young Entrepreneur of the Year Award, has been featured in many publications, including *Black Enterprise magazine,* and was named one of the top 10 people making a global difference in *The Michigan Chronicle.* Ephren's ability to utilize resources allowed him to obtain great wealth at a young age and have once in a lifetime experiences, such as speaking at the White House on the sixth anniversary of the September 11th attacks, and make the largest donation to the oldest black university Cheyney University.

You can learn from Ephren's story by realizing your greatest resources come from gaining knowledge, which can eventually turn into monetary blessings. Increase your swag by opening yourself up to learn and develop new ideas through the resources available to you. Don't get caught up in thinking you need a huge check in order to help you *Go for Yours.*

Use ALL of your TALENTS

"So he who had received five talents came and brought five other talents saying, 'Lord you delivered to me five talents; look, I have gained five more talents beside them.'"
—Matthew 25:20

S OMEONE WITH swag is brave enough to follow one passion, in order to discover more talents. Remember, your talents are related to your purpose and if you don't use them, you are neglecting yourself and the people who will benefit from them. Do your best to use each talent to its fullest potential.

Former Supermodel Tyra Banks is everything but shy when it comes to utilizing her many talents. Before she received her big break in the modeling industry, she was accepted to several universities and had planned to major in film and television, but decided to put this dream on hold in order to pursue a career in modeling.

Tyra made great use of her talent in the world of modeling after she signed with Elite Model Management. When she went to Paris for runway modeling, she was well received by the designers and was booked for 25 runway shows, which is rare for new models. Tyra appeared in *Vogue, Cosmopolitan* and *Elle,* and she was the first African American female to be on the cover of *GQ magazine* and the *Sports Illustrated* swimsuit edition. From print magazines to runway shows, Tyra has excelled in every area.

While modeling, she used her talents to branch into acting and started her television career during the fourth season of *The Fresh Prince of Bel-Air,* where she played the role of Will's best friend Jackie Ames. From there, she went on to the big screen and starred in *Higher Learning, Love and Basketball* and *Coyote Ugly.* Tyra took her talents to a new level when she created the reality show *America's Next Top Model* (ANTM), which premiered in 2003. ANTM is a show where young women compete for a chance to break into the modeling industry, and at the same time, are given the opportunity to become more self-aware through developing positive characteristics, such as confidence and addressing personal issues.

In 2005, Tyra did her last runway show during the Victoria's Secret fashion show. That same year, she took her talents a step further and premiered her talk show *The Tyra Banks Show,* where she talked about self-esteem issues and relationships, gave fashion advice, and featured celebrity interviews. This show awarded her a Daytime Emmy in 2008 and 2009. Her talk show ended in 2010, but repeats of the show continue to remain on the air. Tyra has served as the executive producer for ANTM and *The Tyra Banks Show*—both of which were created under her independent film company Bankable Productions, where she is the CEO.

Tyra has taken her talents and even dabbled in other industries, including the music industry, when she made songs such as *Shake Ya Body,* that had a music video featuring six final contestants on *ANTM,* cycle

2. Tyra also wrote a book, *Modelland,* a book inspired by her real-life experiences. Recently, Tyra went back to her dream of attending college and enrolled in the Owner Management Program at Harvard University's Business School. Tyra seems to understand her talents are related to her purpose and uses them for a greater cause. She is the founder of TZONE foundation, which offers resources to community non-profit organizations.

Since Tyra chooses to use all of her talents, she has worn many hats and holds multiple titles, such as, supermodel, actress, executive producer, CEO, singer, author, and philanthropist. It should be no surprise that in 2009, she was listed in *Forbes magazine* as the highest paid female in primetime television with an income of $30 million.

Discovering your talents helps you grow to become the person you are meant to be. Like Tyra, choose to discover every talent you possess. Take the first step to discover one passion and watch how doors will open.

Don't STOP

"I thought I told you that we won't stop. I thought I told you that we won't stop."
—Diddy, in *Only You*, by 112

SOMEONE WITH swag continues to create more opportunities for themselves by achieving goal after goal. They know that achieving one goal allows them to create more opportunities. For example, starting a non-profit organization could lead to writing a book; singing can turn into acting, and the love for basketball can turn into owning a basketball franchise. When you have finally achieved a goal, *Go for Yours* by pursuing another accomplishment.

When hip-hop mogul, who can also be referred to as the godfather of swag, Sean "Diddy" Combs said, "I thought I told you that we won't stop," he meant it. Whether he decides to go by the name of Puff Daddy, P. Diddy or simply, Diddy, he just won't stop.

Diddy could have considered himself to be successful well over 10 years ago, but he continues to create new, fresh, and exciting opportunities that have built an enterprise, which will last a lifetime. Diddy took a shot in the entertainment industry when he worked as a party promoter, while attending Howard University. With no intentions to stop, he interned at Uptown Records, and at the age of 19, he was their youngest executive, who is noted for the development and signing of Jodeci and Mary J. Blige.

After being fired from Uptown, he continued to move towards his vision and founded the incredible Bad Boy Records. At Bad Boy, he signed prominent artists such as Faith Evans, 112, Mase, and the late, great Notorious B.I.G. When Diddy, who went by "Puffy" at the time, decided to put out his debut album *No Way Out*, his single, *Can't Nobody Hold Me Down,* was number one for six weeks on the *Billboard* 100 and he won a Grammy for the best rap album. This album was released while he was dealing with the tragic death of his good friend Notorious B.I.G., but he refused to stop and released a song dedicated to him on the album, *I'll be Missing You,* which debuted at number one on the *Billboard* 100.

Diddy has made a successful music career that has led to three Grammys and the release of a number of albums:*The Saga Continues, Forever, Press Pla,y* and *The Last Train to Paris*. His musical success does not stop here. Diddy continues to stay relevant in the music industry, as he recently founded the group, Dirty Money, which consists of himself and Singers Dawn Richard and Kalenna Harper.

Diddy's talent is not limited to the studio, as he has been seen acting alongside Halle Berry in the movie, *Monsters Ball,* and he also starred in the television adaption of *Raisin in the Sun,* as well as, in the movies, *Carlito's Way: Rise to Power* and *Get Him to the Greek.* By never stopping, he has also helped people fulfill their dreams through reality shows like, *Making the Band 2, Making Diddy's Band* and *I Wanna Work for*

Diddy. His drive for success allowed him to gain a star on Hollywood Boulevard, and he still hasn't stopped.

For Diddy, it appears he strives to do more than be famous, as he has made successful business ventures, such as the creation of the clothing line Sean Jean and his unforgettable cologne Unforgiveable. He can be credited for the success of the premium vodka Ciroc, for which he played a prominent role in its development. Whether it is opening up an upscale restaurant or making music, Diddy just won't stop. He made an impact in the community when he ran in the New York City Marathon and raised $2 million, and he encouraged young people to vote during the Vote or Die campaign during the 2004 Presidential Election.

In 2005, *Time magazine* noted Diddy as one of the 100 most influential people. He was featured in *Fortune magazine* as one of the 40 Richest People under 40, and he was number one in the list of top ten richest people in hip hop in 2002. In 2010, his estimated worth was $475 million, which made him the richest person in the hip-hop entertainment business. None of this could have happened if Diddy had decided to stop. If it's anyone who deserves to sit around all day, it's Diddy, but he does just the opposite and works even harder. Once you've reached a goal, increase your swag by continuing to work hard. Don't ever stop until you fulfill your purpose.

DRESS for PERCEPTION

"Cool outrageous lovers of uniquely raw style . . ."
–Fonzworth Bentley, *C.O.L.O.U.R.S*

A S MENTIONED before, swag is all about what's on the inside; however, your style and the way you dress can also play an important role in your swag. This does not mean you have to wear the most expensive clothes. Your swag has nothing to do with name brands. Dressing for perception is all about your style. Your style allows you to highlight your personality and what you bring to the table. How you are perceived when people initially meet you is usually how they will remember you. Your appearance plays a huge role in how people treat you and interact with you. If you want them to know you mean business, remember to dress the part in order to play the part. This doesn't mean your style has to be guided by the latest trend, but you should dress the way you want to be perceived. Not everyone can show up to a job interview in a "wife beater" shirt, raggedy jeans, a Members Only jacket, with paint all over their face, and clothes like Will Smith's in the movie, *Pursuit of Happyness,* and still land a job. The way you dress can represent your ability to perform and gives you the confidence to **Go for Yours**.

Recording Artist/Author Derrick Watkins, who people refer to as Fonzworth Bentley, is a perfect model when it comes to dressing for perception. Fonzworth, the former valet and personal assistant to Sean "Diddy" Combs, knew he needed to portray a certain image to work alongside Diddy. It is evident Fonzworth was fully aware of Diddy's image and style, and understood he had to be presentable if he wanted to work for a businessman of Diddy's stature. Although he would be working as Diddy's valet and assistant, Fonzworth had to dress in a way that represented his boss. He obviously knew if Diddy's assistant wasn't dressed for success, then the way people perceived him could possibly change. If Fonzworth didn't dress for the role, he wouldn't have been afforded the opportunity to showcase his talents and abilities that contributed to various career opportunities.

Dressing for perception allowed Fonzworth to give tips in his book, *Advance Your Swagger: How to use Manners, Confidence, and Style,* to get ahead. It also qualified him to teach young, misdirected men how to be gentlemen on the MTV reality show, *From G's to Gents,* and to become a motivational speaker. His keen style has been seen in music videos with Usher, OutKast, and P. Diddy, and on VH1's *Fashion Rocks.*

He started a music career and has worked with notable artists, such as Kanye West and Andre 3000. Fonzworth's love and knowledge for style is represented in his mixtape entitled, *C.O.L.O.U.R.S,* which stands for cool outrageous lovers of uniquely raw style. He shows his love for style in the song *Take it Back,* but also tells us personal stories in the song *Believe It,* featuring Faith Evans, where he shares his story of overcoming a malignant tumor. Through style, Fonzworth created an image for himself that led to a successful career.

Dressing for perception gets you to the role you want to play. Like Fonzworth, make sure you dress in a way that helps create opportunities for yourself. If you feel you don't know how you should dress for the part, dress more conservatively until you are aware of the atmosphere you will be working in. It's better to be overdressed than underdressed. There may come a time when you can get away with wearing whatever you want, but until then, ***Go for Yours*** dressing in a way that is appropriate and presentable and compliments your swag.

CHAPTER 12

GO FOR YOURS
WITH FAITH

"I never really had the classic struggle, I had faith."
–Denzel Washington

Dare to take a LEAP of FAITH

"Go on honey; take a chance."
–Coming to America

HOPEFULLY THE previous chapters have shown you that the most important ingredient you need when you decide to *Go for Yours* is faith. Everyone mentioned in this book had enough faith to follow their dreams. It's easy to say you have faith when you know you have a paycheck coming in every two weeks, where your next meal is coming from, and if you have a place to sleep at night. Your faith gets tested when the paychecks stop coming and you have no idea where your next meal is coming from. Your faith will be tested the most when you decide to go against what seems normal in order to follow whatever it is you are passionate about. But if you learn how to truly rely on your faith, you are setting yourself up for a beautiful and rewarding experience.

Co-Founder of WEEN (Women in Entertainment Empowerment Network), Valeisha Butterfield dared to take a leap of faith when it came to following her dream of working in the entertainment industry. Valeisha's passion for entertainment grew during the progressive days of hip-hop, when artists, such as DJ Jazzy Jeff and the Fresh Prince, LL Cool J, and Salt N Pepa were heavy on the music scene. She recalls watching the *Summertime* video, by DJ Jazzy Jeff and the Fresh Prince, on BET, and wanting to be a part of the creativity behind videos like that. She also appreciated BET because she was able to see people on television who looked like her. Growing up in Wilson, NC, which is filled with traditional jobs, she didn't know about the resources available to break into the entertainment industry.

Valeisha's passion grew as she got older, and when it was time to pursue a college degree, her passion led her to Clark Atlanta University in Atlanta, GA. She attended college at a time when the black entertainment industry was rapidly growing in Atlanta, and people like L.A. Reid and Jermaine Dupri were continuously contributing to its growth. Valeisha spent four years in college majoring in political science, but was determined to find opportunities in the field of entertainment. While in school, she gained experience and built a network in the entertainment industry that solidified her desire to work in the industry and that provided her with opportunities for employment upon graduation.

During her senior year, fear kicked in, and her parents and friends kept telling her she should be more practical in choosing her career.

Valeisha decided to stop chasing her dream, in spite of the job opportunities she received, and moved back to North Carolina to enroll in law school. During her time in law school, she was surrounded by people who were driven, but Valeisha did just enough to get by.

After she completed her first year of law school, Valeisha chose to take a leap of faith and decided to move to New York in order to follow her dream of working in the entertainment industry. She slept on her friend's couch and applied and interviewed for numerous internships. Her faith was tested when she wasn't offered any internships. After two months of not even getting an unpaid internship in the entertainment field, an agent brought her on board as an unpaid intern, and she was referred to a job for HBO. Valeisha worked for HBO Sports and was provided a great salary, while moving up in the ranks, but this still wasn't an industry she was passionate about.

A lightbulb went off one day after seeing Russell Simmons on CNN, and she decided she wanted to reach out to him and tell him why she should work for him. She did her research, found his e-mail address, and sent him a message telling him, in her best four sentences, why she should work for him.

A few weeks later, Russell called her in for a meeting, and she was offered a full-time, unpaid internship. Again, her faith was tested, and she had to make the decision to leave a job that guaranteed a paycheck in order to work for no pay. At this point, her faith was so strong that she left her job immediately and started her internship the next day. Valeisha made the best out of this opportunity. Nine months later, she became a director, and within a year-and-a-half, she became a vice president. This leap of faith opened the door for more opportunities.

Today, she is the co-founder for WEEN (Women in Entertainment Empowerment Network), a non-profit organization committed to supporting, promoting, and defending the balanced, positive portrayal of women in entertainment and society. Today, this organization has 40,000 members worldwide and provides entertainment-based educational programs on health, financial literacy, career development, and personal advancement for young women nationwide. In addition, she received a presidential appointment and served in the Administration of U.S. President Barack Obama from 2009-2011 as the Deputy Director of Public Affairs for International Trade. Valeisha's success can be credited to taking a leap of faith.

Challenge yourself and dare yourself to take a leap of faith. When you approach fear, refuse to let it prevent you from following your dreams and continue to follow the desires of your heart. Take that leap, so you can land in a bundle of opportunities.

Worry about NOTHING; PRAY about EVERYTHING

"Be anxious about nothing, but in everything, prayer and supplication with thanksgiving, let your requests be known unto God."
–Phillipans 4:6

WHEN YOU **Go for Yours** with faith, you have nothing to worry about. This is easier said than done because when you open yourself up to something new and unfamiliar, a feeling of doubt and fear usually follows. For instance, you may have thought about pursuing a goal such as writing a book, but didn't follow through because you didn't want the hassle of finding a publisher or you worried too much about how much time it would take and the amount of money you would have to spend that you don't have.

Instead of worrying, work towards your goal with enough prayer and faith to know your passion will take you exactly where you are supposed to be. When you become brave enough to follow your dream, you will realize the problems you worried about weren't real problems.

Gospel Singer, Songwriter, and Producer Tye Tribbett seemed to do everything, but worry, when he began his gospel music career and started his group

Tye Tribett and Greater Anointing. He may have been fearful about how people were going to perceive his creative way of praising the Lord, but no one would ever know because he entered the gospel music scene with much prayer and an abundance of faith. He believed in his work enough to take the risk of being criticized by conservative Christians—who may not be accepting to an edgier style of gospel music that sometimes had an R&B and hip hop feel. He also opened himself up to be criticized by mainstream artists for using the energy of the R&B and hip hop world to spread the gospel in his songs. Tye brought a new and refreshing anointing to the world of gospel with his songs, such as, "No Way" (The GA Chant), which made it to the *Billboard* Top 10 Gospel Chart. Not worrying about what people thought of him led him to work with an array of gospel artists, including artists in other genres, such as Whitney Houston, Luther Vandross, and Jill Scott.

Tye seemed to remain prayerful on his journey and allowed his faith to lead him on his path to great success. If he spent time worrying about what people would think about his style of music, or how hard the road would be, he wouldn't have produced four albums, been awarded two Stellar Awards or been nominated for three Grammy Awards. His faith gave him the confidence to spread the goodness of God's word, and most of all, introduce more young people to praise and worship through songs, like "Your Blood" and "Keep Me."

Again, Tye relied on his faith when he made the decision to record his fourth studio album *Fresh,* as a solo artist. According to his website, www.tyetribbett. com, Tye went on a 60-day sabbatical from his ministry, and while he was fasting, he received a revelation in Isaiah 43:18-19: "Forget the former things; do not dwell on the past. See, I am doing a new thing." This scripture helped Tye understand he was entering a new season in his life, and instead of worrying about things of the past, he put all his faith in God. In addition to his music, Tye spreads the word of God through his clothing line Fresh Anointing, which consists of trendy t-shirts, and his weekly Bible study sessions Word on the Street: Biblical Teachings on the Kingdom Life.

Like Tye, focus on your purpose, instead of worrying about issues that really don't exist. You will face some challenges along the way, but if you allow worry to get in the way of realizing your dreams, you will be defeated before you even start. When an idea comes to mind, look at it as a gift from God, instead of worrying about how you are going to make things happen.

Your purpose will put you in the RIGHT place at the RIGHT time

"For the vision is yet for an appointed time."
–Habakkuk 2:2

H AVE ENOUGH faith to know your purpose will put you in the right place at the right time. Was there ever a time in your life when being just one minute early or late, or not showing up at all, could have resulted in you missing out on an experience of a lifetime? Usually, these are the times when something extravagant happens. Some people miss these moments because they are too caught up in thinking about *what* they want and *when* they should have it. Too many people are disappointed because they attempted to plan every detail in their life. No matter how hard you try, some things are about being at the right place at the right time.

Gabrielle Union probably knows all about being at the right place at the right time. She started college at the University of Nebraska, where she played on the women's soccer team, and then transferred to Cuesta College in California before she transferred to University of California, Los Angeles (UCLA) to major in Sociology. During her time at UCLA, she interned at the Judith Fontaine Modeling & Talent Agency to earn academic credit. Gabrielle's post-graduation goals were to attend law school, but she was asked by the agency's owner to become a client at the agency when her internship was complete. Gabrielle accepted the offer with the intention to pay off her student loans.

Gabrielle's modeling career took off, and her face was even seen in *Teen Magazine.* During her modeling career, it was soon discovered she could act. Gabrielle landed her first audition and job, without any headshots, on the sitcom *Saved by the Bell: The New Class,* and was given acting roles on *Moesha; Sister, Sister;* and *7th Heaven.* Eventually, she entered the movie scene and landed small roles in the movies *10 Things I Hate About You, Love and Basketball,* and *Two Can Play That Game.* These roles led to larger roles in movies, such as *Bring it On, Daddy's Little Girls, Deliver Us From Eva,* and *Bad Boys II.*

It is obvious Gabrielle was at the right place at the right time, and she was open to new opportunities that didn't necessarily relate to her future goals. Today, she has a flourishing acting career and continues to break barriers, despite the challenges African American actresses face when it comes to landing roles. She has received two Black Reel Awards and a number of BET and Image Award nominations. In addition, she is passionate about contributing to the community, and is a public speaker and advocate for victims of sexual assault.

You may not have whatever it is you are asking for because it may not be your time to receive it, or you are destined to take a different path. The truth of the matter is, you don't know where life will take you. Whatever your plans are, there may be something greater in store for you that you didn't plan for. If you get discouraged because something is not working out in the time you think it should, *Go for Yours* remembering you may not be where you want to be, but you may be exactly where you are supposed to be at the moment.

There is a PLAN just for YOU

"For I know the plans I have for you, declares the Lord,
plans for you to prosper and not harm you,
plans to give you hope and a future."
−Jeremiah 29:11

I T IS easier to have faith when you know there is a plan and purpose for your life. No matter what the situation was before you were put on this earth, there is a reason why you are here now. You will go through many trials and tribulations, and until your purpose is fulfilled, you will continue to survive each hard time. The trials and tribulations you will face may leave you questioning your faith, and even your existence, but it is necessary for you to understand there is a calling on your life that not even you can stop.

Football Player Troy Pascley survived many trials and tribulations that left him with no choice but to believe there is a plan for his life. He grew up in Alliance, OH, and was raised by a single mother. The only images he has of his father during his childhood are vivid memories of him being abusive to his mother and arguing with her over drugs.

By the time he was in the first grade, Troy was considered the man of the house and carried a key around his neck to let himself in the house after school.

Troy's family didn't have luxuries, like television or a phone, and they were sometimes left wondering where their next meal would come from. Their lack of resources brought them closer and made it easier for them to rely on each other.

In the fifth grade, Troy became passionate about football and used the sport to escape what was going on at home. During his teenage years, he lost interest in school and was lucky if he received a 1.0 grade point average (GPA). His relationship with his mother took a turn for the worse when she started to date. He turned to selling drugs and hanging out with the wrong crowd. Troy faced many experiences that could have left him dead or in jail, like being shot at and stealing a car with his cousin. If it weren't for significant people in his life, like his girlfriend, Britney, who is now his wife, and the Suitca's, a family who took him in after he befriended their son on the football team, Troy doesn't know how his life would be. Despite his circumstances, Troy had a 3.8 GPA by his senior year and received over 20 scholarship offers for football.

Troy ended up at the University of Louisville on a football scholarship. During his first year in college, Troy reverted back to his old ways. All he wanted to do was party, drink, and smoke. This led to him earning a .07 GPA one semester and losing interest in football. Troy decided to move closer to home to go to school. Things didn't work out as planned, and he took a job working 12-hour days in a factory. He contacted a coach at the University of Louisville to see if he could return. Troy was given his scholarship back and enrolled back in school.

Troy's life changed when one of his teammates invited him to fellowship with some Christian athletes. After reading a scripture in Ephesians that talked about what it means to imitate God, it made him realize it was by the grace of God that he made it through. Troy gives God all of the credit for his grades going up and graduating from the University of Louisville with a Bachelor's degree in Personal Communications. Since then, he has worked out with 28 NFL teams and is waiting to hear back from one. He is confident God has a perfect plan for his life.

It is important you understand there is a plan for your life. No matter what you are going through, know that it will only last for a season. When you come out of bad situations, you gain strength that will allow you to **Go for Yours** and be wise enough to handle what's next to come.

CHAPTER 13

GO FOR YOURS WITH THE SPIRIT OF A TRAILBLAZER

"Change will not come if we wait for some other person or some other time. We are the ones we've been waiting for. We are the change that we seek."
—Barack Obama

Don't be AFRAID to be the FIRST

"I decided long ago, never to walk in anyone's shadows."
—Whitney Houston, *Greatest Love of All*

T HE MOST unique thing about trendsetters and trailblazers is they decide to do something no one else has done. They do things people may have thought about doing, but were too afraid to take a step that no one else had already taken. There are too many people in our generation who follow the trend, instead of setting it. People tend to wear what everyone else is wearing, go where everyone else is going, and do what everyone else is doing. When it comes to doing something new, most people are afraid to fail.

State Representative Alisha Thomas Morgan set a trend when she became the first African American to serve in the Georgia House of Representatives for Cobb County, and was the youngest female member of the entire Georgia Assembly. While Alisha was not afraid to be the first, there were some people who did not feel she deserved the opportunity. Her first campaign consultant, who once supported her, filed a residency challenge against Alisha, resulting in her being taken off the ballot. Alisha had to appeal this twice before the judge overturned it and she was back on the ballot.

Since this dynamic trailblazer was not afraid to be the first, she opened up numerous opportunities for people and was instrumental in passing the historical bill, the HB 881, which created the Georgia Charter Schools Commission, offering an alternate route for groups and companies seeking to establish charter schools. Alicia launched the Closing the Achievement Gap Campaign in order to identify ways to prepare students in a global market.

Alisha continues to set trends for her peers and was a key player in helping develop the Young Elected Officials Network, a non-profit program dedicated to connecting and supporting progressive elected leaders under the age of 35. Alisha has received many accolades, such as the YWCA Women of Achievement Award and the Champion for Choice Award from the American Federation for Children. She was recognized by *Ebony* magazine as one of the Nation's 30 Leaders under 30 and by *Essence* magazine as one of the 15 women of the "New Power Generation."

Since Alisha was not afraid to be the first, she has changed the lives of many people around her. She continues to work to reform the educational system, which she believes to be outdated. Alisha plans to create a more student-focused system that is more beneficial to students. She also serves on two national boards, Black Alliance for Educational Options and the National Board for Public School Options.

Alisha strongly believes in the Benjamin E. Mayes quote, "*Every person is born into this world to do something distinctive and unique, and if he or she doesn't do it, it will never be done.*" It is evident Alisha believes this to be true in her life because she was not afraid to be the first.

Today, make a decision to be the first. You may have been blessed with a gift no one else has, and if they do have it, they may have been too afraid to use it. You may have to be the first person in your generation to pursue what you want to do. Don't let the fact that no one else has done what you are trying to do get in the way of pursuing your dream. Instead, **Go for Yours** with the heart and spirit of a trailblazer and set a trend for others.

Spread your WINGS and FLY
toward your DREAMS

*"I am riding high, don't want to come down; hope my wings
don't fail me now, and if I can touch the sky, I'd risk to fall
just to know how it feels to fly."*
—Alicia Keys, *How it Feels to Fly*

THERE ARE too many people who have prevented themselves from the best experiences of their lives because they are afraid of flying on a plane. They would rather take a train or bus, or even worse, never leave the town they reside in. In the same aspect, some people are afraid to spread their wings and follow their destination. Their fear of falling prevents them from witnessing some of the greatest experiences of their lives. When it comes to your dreams, make sure you overcome the fear of flying. Someone who has the spirit of a trailblazer is not afraid to fly and they are brave enough to spread their wings and fly to their destination.

Sisters Kelly and Kimberly Anyadike dreamed of flying since they were young children. Both learned how to fly at Tomorrow's Aeronautical Museum, which is a museum in Compton, CA, founded by Chief Pilot Robin Petgrave. According to Robin's website, <u>www.tamuseum.org</u>, Robin's mission is to, "encourage youth involvement in aviation as an alternative to drugs, gang violence, and other self-destructive activities."

On Kelly's 16th birthday, she made it into the Guinness Book of World Records for being the youngest African American female to fly solo in four different fixed-wing aircrafts on the same day. Kimberly was so passionate about learning to fly that she washed airplanes and performed tasks to earn museum dollars that she traded in for flight lessons. Inspired by the Tuskegee Airmen, she became the youngest African American female to pilot a private airplane from coast to coast.

When it comes to flying, both sisters soar in various areas. While in high school, Kelly completed college level art, speech, and sign language courses. She served as a junior lifeguard and took an active interest in surfing and golf. She participated in the Lula Washington Dance Academy, in Los Angeles, CA, where she learned tap dance and ballet. She learned how to read music and still plays the piano and flute.

Kimberly also served as a junior lifeguard and learned how to surf. At Lula Washington Academy, she took ballet, hip hop, and tap dance classes. She has embraced her musical talents and learned to play the piano, violin and guitar. Her overall goal is to become a cardiovascular surgeon, with a pilot's license. Both girls excel in academics and volunteer in their local community. Because the Anyadike sisters weren't afraid of flying, they have approached some of the most valuable experiences of their lives and are on a path to greatness.

It is important for you to remember your fear of flying can set limitations on your dreams. It is true that when you fly, you will face turbulence and encounter some storms, but continue to spread your wings and soar above adversity in order to **Go for Yours**.

Follow your OWN DREAMS

"Don't listen to what nobody say, and don't let nobody turn you away when you got big dreams."
—Bow Wow, *Big Dreams*

R EMEMBER, EVERYONE is not going to believe in you and support your dreams. The reason why they don't does not always stem from people wanting you to fail, but from people who are looking out for your best interests, and they don't want to see you fail.

When you **Go for Yours** with the mindset of a trailblazer you are pursuing something no one else in your family or circle of friends has even thought of. They might think you are crazy for wanting to obtain some of the things you desire because their definition of stability has nothing to do with what you want to do. There are some successful people who wouldn't have made it if they allowed the fact their parents refused to pay their tuition because they didn't major in a degree they viewed as successful, or if they had let someone stop them from moving to a new city that was filled with amazing opportunities.

When it came to following a dream, Author and Motivational Speaker Bert Gervais learned the importance of pursuing his own dream. Bert's family came from Haiti, one of the poorest countries in the world, and they had a strong desire for him to be successful. He spent his college career at Binghamton University in Binghamton, NY, where he majored in history and was a student leader, activist, and entrepreneur. Bert's plan was to follow his parent's desire for him to attend law school. He experienced a lot of stress when he realized he no longer wanted to be a lawyer and wanted to pursue business. Stress and anxiety caused him to develop a rare disease and almost die, which led him to spend Thanksgiving of 2006 in the hospital. When he recovered, Bert had to deal with the fact that he was behind in his schedule for graduating from college, and even worse, he was behind in pursuing his dreams.

After graduation, Bert ended up with a job in corporate America. He was unhappy with his job and felt he had a higher calling on his life, but continued to work—not wanting to disappoint his family. Eventually, there was a cutback on employees and he was laid off. Embarrassed to tell his family and friends, Bert got up every day as if he was going to a regular nine to five job, and would end up at a friend's house, who was the only one who knew he no longer had a job. This experience led him to writing his first book, *Who's in Your Top Hive: A Guide to Finding Your Success Mentors*, which he wrote out of his friend's basement.

Following his own dreams allowed Bert to become a best-selling author and award-winning entrepreneur—all before his 25th birthday. He is known as, "The Mentor Guy," and is one of the most in-demand young professional speakers. Bert has been a panelist for Global Entrepreneurship Week, which broadcasts to over seven million people in 80 countries throughout the world. He has spoken in over 30 cities across the United States, alongside the U.S. Department of Labor and the National Chamber of Commerce. He has appeared in publications, like *USA Today* and *Young Money Magazine*. Bert learned the importance of following his own dreams and passion, and now travels across the country to share his experience with other young people.

When it comes to following your dream, make sure you spend time pursuing something you are passionate about. If you do not receive support from your friends and family, surround yourself with people who share the same interests and can offer advice and support. When you become successful, you will see the same people who were scared for you will be the same people praising you for your success and recognizing you for the trailblazer you are.

PROFIT from being DIFFERENT

"It's not about wanting to be different, I am different."
—Terrell Owens, CNBC's *America's Black Class*

U NFORTUNATELY, WE live in a generation where it is cool to be like everyone else. When someone dares to be different they are looked at as being a nerd or weirdo. Trailblazers are brave people, who step out and do something that is against what everyone else is doing.

Soul Violinist Lee England, Jr. made it look cool to play an instrument that most people around him were not checking out. He was introduced to the violin at the tender age of six and quickly developed a love/hate relationship with it. Lee recalls picking up the violin and quickly putting it back down. He went as far as trying to convince his parents something was wrong with his violin because it didn't sound like he thought it should when he played it. Lee asked his parents if he could quit, and his father told him he could quit only if he practiced 15 minutes per day. Eventually, 15 minutes turned into 30, 30 minutes turned into an hour and his desire to quit playing turned into a desire to play more.

Lee was classically trained to play the violin, but developed his own style that he considers to be a combination of Rhythm and Blues, Gospel, Jazz, Hip Hop, and Symphonic Soul. Lee played the violin throughout grade school, but was rarely teased because of his love for basketball and a childhood friend who used his popularity to stand up for Lee anytime he was ridiculed. Lee attempted to hide his love for the violin behind the game of basketball. If anyone asked him what he wanted to do when he grew up, he would quickly reply, "play basketball."

Lee's interest in the violin became a secret love affair while attending SIU, where he received a Bachelor's degree in Music Business, Music Performance, and Music Education. He spent more time on his school's recreation center's basketball court than playing the violin because he felt the violin overshadowed him as a man. Not many people knew he was a concertmaster in the orchestra until he decided to enter the school's talent show and play the violin. Lee prides himself for winning this show because he was able to show people how he makes the violin look cool, and this was the last time his father saw him play before he passed away. Soon after the talent show, Lee went on to win first place in a classical competition.

Not allowing himself to get caught up in being different, Lee has graced the stage with the likes of Stevie Wonder, Eric Roberson, and T-Pain. He has toured with R&B Artist K'Jon and opened up for artists, such as Anthony Hamilton, Ryan Leslie, and MC Lyte. Lee participated as the only violinist on the MTV show *Making His Band,* a show created in order to make a band for Sean "Diddy" Combs. He enjoys each opportunity and gets the most joy out of his street performances, where he has captivated audiences and developed great relationships.

Today, Lee has an endorsement from NBA Basketball Legend Michael Jordan and can be seen at Michael Jordan's events playing the violin in a custom made Jordan tuxedo that matches the greatness that comes from his violin. He also used his passion to pay it forward when he taught kids at a school on the west side of Chicago and served as their only music teacher. His experience working with the kids motivated them to want to make the violin look cool, just like he does. Lee has not seen half of what is yet to come, but since he was brave enough to try something different, he is in for a great reward.

Go for Yours knowing it is okay to be different from those around you. If you have a quality that may be different from what everyone else is doing, embrace it, because it will make you stand out from the rest and can eventually bring you great profit. You can't profit from being the same as everyone else.

CHAPTER 14

Go for Yours NOW

"Get up, don't sit back. Get up, if you wanna get there.
Clocks don't stop, and time won't wait."
–Mary Mary, *Get Up*

ONE OF the reasons why I chose the title ***Go for Yours*** is because I wanted to encourage people to go after what is already rightfully theirs. It's yours because you were given a special talent,which you are entitled to use. As you continue on your path to follow your dreams, you will face many trials and tribulations, but you must remember you are the only one who can hold you back. The obstacles that come your way are not strong enough to stop you from reaching your dreams. You can only be stopped if you allow your trials and tribulations to hinder you.

Go for Yours being bold in your walk, work diligently towards your goal, and have enough faith to know that you will reach your destination. Enjoy every moment and embrace the struggle, while knowing the hard times you face are shaping you into the person you are destined to be.

I want you to remember the significance of every person mentioned in ***Go for Yours,*** such as the singer and songwriter Ne-yo, who went for his with no excuses by letting nothing or nobody stop him. In the same capacity as Jerome Boykin, don't get caught up in the superficial definition of success. Instead, live by your own definition of success and use it to create your own opportunities similar to Sherhara.

When you become discouraged, think of Jewelry Designer Enovia Bedford, who used her passion to follow her dreams. Remember, you will face difficult people along the way, but like Soulja Boy and 50 Cent, use negative people and haters as a motivator to work even harder. When faced with competition, recall Beyonce, Jay-Z, or Terrance J, who didn't let a little competition scare him away from achieving their goals.

If you approach a situation that seems impossible, think of the quote by Pharrell Williams, *"If you look in the sky and you don't see your dream, man, don't feel defeated."* You will become exhausted from the hard work you are putting in, but refer to Trey Songz, who goes hard every day, and Diddy, who doesn't stop. When your hard work doesn't produce the results you are looking for, turn on one of my favorite Donnie McClurkin songs, and remind yourself to "stand" in the midst of your troubles.

Whenever you feel like giving up, take a step back and remind yourself how great you are. Like Mic Barber, know what you bring to the table and be confident in the fact your talent serves a special purpose. As you continue on your walk, refer to Jeremiah 29:11: *For I know the plans I have for you, declares the Lord, plans for you to prosper and not harm you, plans to give you hope and a future.*

When it comes to following your dreams, remember anything is possible at any time. Create your own opportunity and ***Go For Yours*** now! Don't sit on your talent or purpose, but start working toward your destiny so your story can be told in the next edition of ***Go for Yours***!

AUTHOR'S STORY

"You don't know my story,
all the things that I've been through.
You can't feel my pain,
what I had to go through to get here."
–Bishop Larry Trotter & The Sweet Holy Spirit Combined
Choirs, *My Worship is for Real*

S INCE I wrote a book that features the stories of many young people, it is only fitting that I share mine. As a young child, I always knew I wanted to help people. I looked up to my mother, who was a social worker at the time, and I wanted to be just like her. Whenever someone would ask me what I wanted to be when I grew up, I would reply, "a social worker."

As I grew older, I went through many phases, and my desire to become a social worker changed to wanting to be a lawyer, to a dental assistant, and even a news anchor. All I knew was that I wanted to work with people. I was taught at an early age, the importance of helping others. One of my fondest memories of helping people was volunteering at the nursing home my mother worked at and going with my grandmother to pray for the sick and shut-in.

I grew up in a predominately white town, DeKalb, Illinois with very few blacks, where I experienced failure, hurt, and disappointment. Anyone who knew me growing up knew I was shy, quiet, and timid. I rarely stuck up for myself and was very sensitive. My dad often jokes with me because he thought I was going to be a "softy" when I cried because my favorite basketball player, B.J. Armstrong, was traded from the Chicago Bulls.

Growing up in a town filled with racism and discrimination, I can recall being called derogatory names from my fellow students as early as the third grade. I remember my second grade teacher not wanting to teach me how to write in cursive because she claimed it was hard for her to teach a left-handed child. I was young, but I knew I was not the only "lefty" in the class, and her not wanting to teach me how to write in cursive had more to do with my skin color, than me being left handed. This was the first time I felt discriminated by my teachers, and it definitely wasn't my last. I never had a black teacher, and it wasn't until my senior year in high school that I had a teacher who believed in me.

I didn't have support from my school, but I grew up with parents who were supportive in everything I did. My parents only had two children, both girls, and my dad was determined to have us in sports. I played volleyball and basketball and always ended up on the B-team. When I tried track and field, I would finish last. No matter what, my father was always present cheering me on. As much as it bothered me that I wasn't good in basketball, I focused on my brand new Fila Grant Hill gym shoes, and the fact I was number 10, like B.J. Armstrong. I ended up leaving the sports to my sister, Tiffany, who excelled in basketball, soccer, and track. Since I couldn't play sports, I tried out for pom-poms and cheerleading in high school, but I was immediately cut in both after try-outs.

It was then that I became uninterested in school. I went from being an A-B student to getting D's and F's. I would fail to turn in assignments and projects, and refused to study for a test. It wasn't until my senior year when I finally got my act together, but by then, it was too late. My grades were not good enough to get into a four-year college and my ACT score was pretty low. By that time, I didn't even know what I wanted to go to college for. All I knew is, with two parents, who both held master's degrees, I was going to somebody's college. During my time of trying to figure things out, I recall my government teacher, Mr. Khaler, telling me I was going to be a senator one day. I remember looking at him like he was crazy because I was getting a C in his class! While I was not at all interested in wanting to be a senator, it was obvious he saw me as a leader.

Because my grades were so low, I went to a junior college in Southern Illinois for two years before I transferred to Illinois State University (ISU). It was at ISU, where I truly discovered my leadership abilities. I joined student organizations and pledged a sorority, Delta Sigma Theta, Sorority, Incorporated. I decided to major in Community Health Education. I saw myself working with people and helping them change their unhealthy behaviors. I think I also chose this major because my mom had her Masters in Public Health and was working as a health educator. Again, I wanted to be like my mother.

Instead of working as a health educator, I found a job in the field of social work, working with families whose children were in the foster care system. Tired of working with people who put in absolutely no effort in regaining custody of their children, I enrolled in graduate school at NIU. I can credit pursuing my Masters Degree in Higher Education to two people. One was the advisor of my sorority, Gina Lee, who served as one of my mentors. She inspired me to want to work with college students. The other person was my mentor and sorority sister, Lametra Curry, who made me sit down at her desk and not get up until I finished my mission statement for the application process.

When I was accepted into graduate school, I felt I finally knew what it was I wanted to do, which was work with students in order to help them discover their passion and become great leaders. I also wanted to become a vice president of student affairs, or even become a president at a university. After receiving my master's degree, I received a job as Assistant Director of Diversity and Leadership at a private university in Chicago. I absolutely loved my job. For the first time, I was able to see how nearly every student I encountered was encouraged by me. They would repeat things they heard me say and were inspired by, and looked up to me, as a mentor.

I worked as hard as I could to model the Russell Simmons quote, *"If you learn late, pass it on to others so they can learn early, it's a step process."* My experience at the university made me realize I was called to do more than work at a university. I wanted to reach out and motivate as many people as I could. I didn't want people to go through as much as I did in order to find out what they were called to do. This experience led me to writing **Go for Yours**. I am not sure where this path will take me, but I am confident it will lead me on a path to motivate and encourage others during my journey.

CREATION OF GO FOR YOURS

N EW YEARS of 2010 I had one of the most significant
experiences of my life. I have always brought in
the beginning of the year with a new vision, but I felt
something would be different about 2010. For the first
time, I decided to leave Chicago, IL, and bring in the
year in a different state.

My friend Tiara Tucker, and I spent our New Year
in one of the hottest cities in the country, Atlanta, GA.
When I got off the plane, I went to pick up our reserved
vehicle. While at the car rental business, I noticed
a blue convertible Mustang with our name on it. I
quickly called Tiara to see if she wanted to upgrade. It
was freezing in Atlanta, but we didn't care; we wanted
to bring in the New Year with some style! I now realize,
this upgrade was just the beginning of many more
upgrades to come in my life.

This trip was filled with fun and various learning
experiences. We hung out at my favorite spot, Straits;
a restaurant owned by Ludacris, visited family and
friends; and went to places, like the historical Martin
Luther King, Jr. Museum, his childhood home, and
Ebenezer Baptist Church. Although it was about 20
degrees on New Years Day, we drove around with

the convertible top down and the heat blasting, while enjoying the moment.

During that trip, we spoke something powerful into our lives. We declared 2010 would be a year of self-awareness. We both knew God was going to reveal to us our passion and our purpose, and we believed the best was yet to come. We made a pact to keep track of our year and share with each other the self-awareness moments we would experience, while finding our passion. On my flight from Atlanta back to Chicago, I began to write down quotes and decided I wanted to write and publish a book of quotes. When I returned home, I shared the idea with Tiara, and she agreed to be the editor.

After sharing my idea, I then contacted my friend, Randee Drew, who always had powerful quotes on his Facebook page, and asked if he would like to partner with me on this project. Randee was very excited to be a co-author, but as my ideas began to grow, he and I agreed this was a project I should do solo. *Go for Yours* started out as one of the quotes for the book, but I felt it was a powerful title. I recall my good friend, Anthony "Ant P" Peterson, telling me, *"Go for Yours,"* in a particular situation I faced in college. I never went for mine in that situation, but those words stayed with me. What started out as a few pages of handwritten quotes scrawled in my journal, rapidly grew into a compilation of inspirational mantras and stories of successful young African American people who model the *Go for Yours* lifestyle.

Initially, I started writing in January of 2010 and planned to publish my book by November of that same year. I know God laughed at those plans. One day, I shared some of my material with my maternal grandmother, and she prayed over it and asked God to take the book higher and higher and higher. I also shared my book with my paternal grandmother during her last days. I strongly believe when she entered the gates to heaven, she asked God to lead me on the path to finishing my book. Therefore, I give much credit for the success that lies ahead of me to both of my grandmothers.

My desire to create **Go for Yours** developed into a calling to change the lives and attitudes of everyone I encountered. As my vision continued to evolve, I crossed paths with people whose lives and success stories fit the **Go for Yours** mold. Each person mentioned in this book possesses a quality I admire and a story I want to share with as many people as possible. I strongly believe they were handpicked by God to be featured in the book, and the vision is greater than me.

I was convinced **Go for Yours** was meant to be when Tiara and I planned another trip the year after we went to Atlanta. This time, the two of us went to Los Angeles, CA, during the Grammy and NBA All-Star weekends.

While we were out, we would spot people that I had already created stories for in the book. I remember talking to Common and telling him about the book. He congratulated me and wished me luck. We also spotted and talked to other famous people, such as Fonzworth Bentley, Ne-yo, and Nick Cannon, and told them about the book. The fondest memory was when Tiara and I met Beyoncé, and I attempted to tell her about the book. She probably wouldn't recall because the two of us were so excited to see her that we were both rambling in her ear due to our extreme excitement. These small, yet significant moments, made me believe more in my dream.

Every encounter was not successful. I approached people who didn't believe in my book, or just weren't interested. I remember setting up various interviews with people I wanted to feature in the book, only for them to be cancelled. My biggest disappointment was when my brand new computer, with all of my written material, was stolen while I was in Los Angeles. I still didn't get discouraged because I knew that obstacles were part of the territory of going for mine. A month after I received my new computer, the hard drive crashed, and although I didn't lose everything, I had to go back and redo all of my edits, which delayed the date I turned in my manuscript.

Furthermore, I started writing this book while I had a full-time job. I loved my job, but wasn't happy because of the atmosphere I was working in. I found myself stressed out from work and praying for my situation to get better. I faced a life-changing experience when I went to visit my cousin Lamel's girlfriend, Joy, who was in the hospital fighting cancer. I would often visit Joy when she came to Chicago for her chemotherapy, but this visit was different. Instead of seeing the optimistic, fun and bubbly person I shared great conversations with, Joy was on a breathing machine fighting for her life. During my visit, she took her last breath right before my eyes. At that moment, I realized life was too precious to spend it doing something that wasn't fulfilling. Soon after, I quit my job in order to start a new chapter in my life.

Although my job ended abruptly, I was able to take everything I learned from it. I was confident I would be an inspiration to people because of the students I had worked with who still call, text, and tweet me telling me, "*Go for Yours!*" I left that job behind me, but I took with me one of the greatest friendships I developed while going for mine. While I was working, I contacted the Grammy Award-winning artist Malik Yusef to perform at the school. I was a fan of his work and wanted him to perform during Black History Month. Little did he know, I had planned to slip him my book so he could read it, be inspired, and tell his celebrity friends about it.

Because my heart and intentions were good, God took my vision to another level. Malik gave me an opportunity to work with him on his team, and I eventually became his assistant. I could not believe that while going for mine, I was given the opportunity to work for an artist I admired. Through this encounter, we developed a great relationship, and he is now the big brother I always wanted. My experience working for Malik also contributed to the growth of *Go for Yours*.

I wouldn't change the good or bad experiences I encountered during this journey because they made me stronger and pushed me to work even harder. Overall, my experience has showed me that God can fulfill your dreams far beyond your imagination. Now, my dreams have become a little bigger. I see myself as an author of more books, a motivational speaker, and the first African American from DeKalb, IL, to be well known.

I use my story as a testimony for you to realize that when there is a calling on your life, nothing can get in the way from achieving what you are called to do. Your purpose is so powerful that not even you can stop it. You may already know exactly what your purpose is, or you may stumble across it. You may not find out what it is until you experience loss, failure, or disappointment. Whatever the case, your purpose will be revealed, and when it is, you will be blessed with unduplicated success.

ACKNOWLEDGEMENTS

W HEN I chose to follow my dream and write a book, there were so many people along the way who inspired and encouraged me to move towards my goal. I would like to thank everyone who believed in me especially during the times I didn't believe in myself.

I must first start off by giving all of my thanks to God who carefully ordered my steps along my journey to completing this project.

To my parents, Beverly and Leonard McCall, thank you for your encouragement and believing in me when I decided to step out on faith. Mom, thank you for showing me the true definition of a virtuous woman. Dad, you continue to show me the importance of putting God and my family first. To my little big sister Tiffany, I have learned so much from you. I admire your strength and the fact that you go for yours not caring what others think, but aiming to please God. To my Grandma Candias, words cannot express my gratitude towards you. You prayed that God would take my vision higher and higher and higher and that's exactly what happened. Thank you for sharing your wisdom. To my Grandpa Charles, I love you. To my grandparents, Lucille McCall and Herbert Walker who did not live to see me publish my book but left a legacy behind, I have taken the torch and plan to leave a legacy of my own. Auntie Ginger, I look up to you so much! You have taught me the importance of having a giving spirit and I thank you for that. To my uncles, Herbert Walker, Roy Walker, Mickey McCall, Charles McCall, Victor McCall, Dwight McCall, and Darryl McCall. To the rest of my aunts and uncles, I love each and every one of you.

To my cousins who are more like siblings: Kevin Kirk, Lorenzo Garth Jr., Aundrea McCall, Conola McCall, Britney Sivels, Lamel Tolbert, Darien Walker, Eileen Walker, Terrance Walker, and Ebonie Wilmington; and to the rest of my cousins I pray this book inspires you to go for yours!

To my childhood friends whom I consider family that I share great memories with and who still take out the time to check on me: Gretchen Admonis, Ericka Herd, Tiffany Herd (thanks for your help), Cedric Little, Natasha Lippi, Yamira Montoya, Taisha Murrell, Nekoba Mutima, Masai Mwinzi, Monique Shered, Derris Hawkins-Smith, Ronnie Tucker, Bahati "Lydia" Walls, Jessica Webb, Jasmine West, Jason Wright, and the rest of my DeKalb family.

To my college buddy, Anthony "Ant P" Peterson, thank you for being the first person to tell me "Go for Yours!" To the rest of my college friends, Kameisha Armstead, Yaisa Watts-Braithwaite, Chifana Colbert, Tiffany Pryor, Pamela Richmond, and Brandin Stephenson.

To my good friends who encouraged me along the way and consistently motivated me during my trials and tribulations of making it through this project, Andre Brown, Charlene Carruthers, Jarquetta Edgeston, Niesha Jefferson,Brandon Lance McCollum, Rashida Olayiwola, and Jimmy Prude.

To my Sorors of Delta Sigma Theta Sorority, Inc, all of my Theta Delta Sorors, my line sisters of D.S.S.E.P.I.T.O.M.E.8 Ebonee Sawyer, Nadine Taylor, Candace Hansford, Keli Avery, Jennifer Stroud, Tiara Tucker and Sarena Newby. Each and every one of you motivated me and shared your talents with me during this project. It's time to really show them what the "New Fine Line" is made of. To my Delta family: Alicia Williams, Andrea Stubblefield and Jillian McLeod. To my Sorors who motivated me, helped me and connected me with people during this project: Tashaunda Anderson, Lametra Curry Treveda Redmond, Tia Salmon, Kimberly Wilson, and Tracy Carr-Wright.

To the students who helped me realize the impact I have on young people: Darryl Brown, Markia Kelly, Leeza Steward, Otis Rucker, and Alexis Ware. Thanks for consistently telling me "Go for Yours" and believing in this project!

To everyone who took the time out to share their personal story with me: Latoya Ausley, Mic Barber, Enovia Bedford, Jerome Boykin, Lorielle Broussard, Valeisha Butterfield, Randee Drew, Lee England Jr., Bert Gervais, Joshua Mercer, Kari Miller, Alisha Thomas Morgan, Troy Pascley, Dana Todd Pope, David D.

Robertson, Sherhara, Marcus Spencer, Lavelle Sykes, Traxster, Rod West, Garrett Wolfe, and Malik Yusef. Most of all, thank you for going for yours. To the people mentioned in this book through quotes and examples, I would like to thank you for showing the world it is possible to follow your dreams.

To the Go for Yours team: Antonio Berry, Diondre King, Jeremiah Myles, Jamie Smothers, Tonja Thigpen. Some of you didn't know me at all, but you believed so much in this project and were willing to share your talents. Thank you for helping me spread the message and believing in me. Thanks to everyone who helped with the photo shoot commercial, and supported the Go for Yours events.

To my editor and friend Tiara, thank you so much for your patience and for showing me I don't have to use the word "that" in every sentence. Seriously, I appreciate your hard work and dedication to this project. Being my editor and friend was not easy, you motivated and uplifted me while spending countless hours editing.

Those not mentioned you have touched my heart in some shape or form. I also would like to thank everyone whom I have never met, but took the time out to read this book I hope you were inspired.

INDEX

CPSIA information can be obtained at www.ICGtesting.com
Printed in the USA
BVOW011721251111

276778BV00001B/26/P